Quick Insights into Lancang-Mekong Cooperation: Celebrating Successes

T0418366

www.royalcollins.com

Understanding Regional
Cooperation in Asia Book Series

Quick Insights into Lancang-Mekong Cooperation: Celebrating Successes

Series Editors: Lu Guangsheng and Feng Yue

Editor: Lu Guangsheng

Books Beyond Boundaries

ROYAL COLLINS

Understanding Regional Cooperation in Asia Book Series

Quick Insights into Lancang-Mekong Cooperation: Celebrating Successes

Series Editors: Lu Guangsheng and Feng Yue

Editor: Lu Guangsheng

Translated by: Gao Fengxiang, Lu Mengdi, Li Yue, and Wang Wenpu

Proofread by: Mark Jonathan Harris

First published in 2025 by Royal Collins Publishing Group Inc.

Groupe Publication Royal Collins Inc.

550-555 boul. René-Lévesque O Montréal (Québec) H2Z1B1 Canada

Original edition © Yunnan Education Publishing House

ISBN: 978-1-4878-1298-0

To find out more about our publications, please visit www.royalcollins.com.

Contents

Editor's Note

Hi, This Is the Lancang-Mekong Cooperation

The year 2016 was destined to leave an extremely special and important mark in history, because, from this year onwards, a new phrase has been introduced into China's diplomatic dictionary, that is the Lancang-Mekong Cooperation.

On March 23, 2016, at the scene of the First LMC Leaders Meeting, the Chinese Premier stood side by side with the leaders of the five Mekong countries. Leaders from the six countries slightly tilted the bamboo tubes in their hands, and the water of the Lancang-Mekong River flowed out and then converged into one. The ceremony announced the official launch of this new sub-regional cooperation mechanism. Meanwhile, it was unanimously decided among the leaders of the six countries to build a peaceful and prosperous Lancang-Mekong community with a shared future.

The LMC has been promoted by the intersection of history and reality. The Lancang River, which originates from the Tanggula Mountains in Qinghai, China, is called the Mekong River after it flows out of China from Xishuangbanna. With a total length of 4,880 kilometers, the Lancang-Mekong River flows through

China, Myanmar, Laos, Thailand, Cambodia, and Vietnam, and finally into the South China Sea via Ho Chi Minh City in Vietnam. The six countries are closely connected by the same river and have been naturally bonded by the river since ancient times. With their friendship passed down from generation to generation, the six countries have become natural cooperative partners and close friendly neighbors of each other.

As an ancient Chinese saying goes, "The highest goodness is like water, which benefits all things and does not compete." It denotes that since water has an open and inclusive nature, it nourishes all things, but it does not compete with any of them. The saying vividly interprets how the LMC is rooted in the traditional friendship of the six countries and established on the basis of their common interests, and that it is a choice made by all the six countries to share the same breath, the same destiny, and the fruits of development. President Xi Jinping said, "The LMC has achieved fruitful results since its inception in 2016. It has demonstrated a 'Lancang-Mekong speed and efficiency,' and fostered a Lancang-Mekong culture of equality, sincerity, mutual assistance, and affinity." As the result of the diligent irrigation that has transpired among the six countries, the LMC has grown vigorously, blossoming and bearing wonderful fruits. It has gone through the phases of nurturing and rapid expansion to enter a new stage of comprehensive development, injecting "spring water" into the development of the six countries, and setting a fine example for building a community with a shared future for humankind.

Leading the General Direction for the LMC Based on Mutual Trust

It is necessary to maintain frequent reciprocal visits with neighboring countries. President Xi Jinping attaches great importance to neighborhood diplomacy. He visited the five Mekong countries dozens of times and met and talked with the state leaders to promote the relations between China and the five Mekong countries to transform into continuous development by making the neighboring countries truly feel China's goodwill and sincerity. Chinese Premier attended all the previous LMC Leaders' Meetings and jointly drew up blueprints for the LMC with leaders of the five Mekong countries. The six countries have been making active efforts in building a peaceful and prosperous Lancang-Mekong community with a shared future, with China-Cambodia, China–Laos, China-Myanmar, China-Thailand, and China-Vietnam communities with a shared future being established one after another. Since the inception of the LMC, a multi-level and wide-ranging cooperative framework has been established, including Leaders' Meetings, Foreign Ministers' Meetings, Senior Officials' Meetings, and working group meetings; the Five-Year Plan of Action on the LMC (2018–2022 and 2023–2027) were was formulated, while the plan in areas such as water resources, agriculture, and poverty reduction has been actively implemented; planning on cooperation in the cross-border economy, production capacity, and connectivity is being developed; and an LMC framework "guided by leaders and underpinned by all-round cooperation and broad participation" has been deeply rooted in people's minds.

Working Toward Common Development and Injecting New Momentum Into the LMC

Great truths are always simple, and one of them is that actions speak louder than words. Based on the philosophy of development first, equal consultation, pragmatism and efficiency, and openness and inclusiveness, the LMC has been implemented with solid steps and sounds like a beautiful symphony of mutual respect. With priority given to cross-border economic cooperation, the LMC has vigorously promoted economic and trade exchanges among the six countries, bringing continuous growth of their economic aggregates and the constant improvement of their level of economic and social development and laying a solid foundation for their launch of the Regional Comprehensive Economic Partnership (RCEP). The efficient flow of visitors, logistics, and information. In addition, the China–Laos Railway officially commenced operations, the China-aided Myanmar train carriage project was successfully completed, and a number of other infrastructure connectivity projects have been completed in succession in a high-standard and sustainable manner to benefit people's livelihood from the Mekong countries, such as the first urban light rail project in Vietnam, undertaken by a Chinese company, and the new terminal building of Suvarnabhumi Airport in Thailand, and these have injected lasting momentum into the development of the local regions. Facing a weak recovery and relatively high inflation level of the world economy since 2023, the Lancang-Mekong countries have been working closely to upgrade the quality of cooperation by promoting regional interconnection and expanding co-development spaces, which has boosted the efficient flow of visitors, logistics, and information.

Building a People-to-People Bridge for the LMC

Like the ever-flowing Lancang-Mekong River, friendship among the six Lancang-Mekong countries has been maintained in a stable state. With the belief of having a "shared river and shared future," the six countries have joined hands to achieve common prosperity, fostering a Lancang-Mekong culture featuring "equal treatment, sincerity, and a family-like atmosphere." Based on the principle of being people-oriented, through the implementation of specific projects, the LMC has been committed to building a beautiful homeland for the local region and has been welcomed and recognized by the local people. The China-East Asia Poverty

Reduction Demonstration Cooperation Technical Assistance Project initiated by China was implemented in six pilot villages in Cambodia, Laos, and Myanmar, helping the local villages to glow with new vitality. The second phase of the rural water supply project in Cambodia was launched, addressing the problems of having a shortage of drinking water sources and clean water and sanitation for rural people in Cambodia. The "Sun Village" project introduced solar photovoltaic technology and equipment to villages in Cambodia and Myanmar, lighting up happy lives for the local villagers … Facing the severe challenge brought by the COVID-19 pandemic, the six countries have never ceased their exchanges and cooperation in social and cultural fields, which are represented by the Lancang-Mekong Youth Training Camp for Innovation and Entrepreneurship, and the Forum on Women Issues in the Lancang-Mekong River Basin, demonstrating the amazing vitality of the LMC.

The LMC has yielded a Lancang-Mekong speed that features "progress every day, results every month, and new stages every year." Such a splendid "blossoming of the LMC" is worth discovering, describing, and recording. To this end, focusing on the "3 + 5 + X" cooperation framework of the LMC and starting from the three pillars and the five cooperative areas, this book intends to introduce the planning, implementation, and accomplishments of the LMC. After reading this book, the readers will get to know how the LMC has taken root and blossomed in the fields of connectivity, production capacity, cross-border economy, water resources, agriculture, and poverty reduction, how it has produced a prosperous Lancang-Mekong region based on collaboration among the six countries, and how it has demonstrated its powerful force in promoting the building of a community with a shared future for this region.

In addition, with the use of pictures, data, and words, this book explores the LMC in a visible, perceptible, and understandable manner so as to bring more people to understand the content and the significance of the LMC, know about the dreams of the Chinese people and the people of the five Mekong countries, understand how the dreams of the Lancang-Mekong countries are closely related, and realize that the LMC has become an important platform to promote the joint construction of a community with a shared future for the Lancang-Mekong countries.

Sharing the same river for over one thousand years, the six countries have developed close bonds and shared dreams toward the construction of a wonderful future. No matter how the international situation changes, China will always act as a trustworthy and reliable neighbor, friend, and partner of the five Mekong countries. At a new historical starting point, the six countries will take advantage of the momentum and work hand in hand to promote the LMC to open a new chapter and accelerate the construction of a closer Lancang-Mekong community with a shared future.

A Blueprint for Cooperation Connected by Mountains and Rivers

The Lancang-Mekong River flows through the mountains and rivers of China, Myanmar, Laos, Thailand, Cambodia, and Vietnam, which not only naturally connects the six countries together but also brings about people-to-people affinity among their cultures. As the first sub-regional cooperation mechanism in the river basin where the six countries negotiated, co-constructed, and shared results, the LMC has flourished since its inception and has become one of the most prominent sub-regional cooperative mechanisms with the most vitality and developmental potential.

Originating from the River, the LMC Has Flourished since Its Inception

A River That Connects the Development Dreams of the Six Countries

With a total length of 4,880 kilometers, the Lancang-Mekong River meanders through China, Myanmar, Laos, Thailand, Cambodia, and Vietnam, serving as a natural link to "connect the six countries with the same river." People sharing the same river have multiplied there for generations, giving birth to distinctive cultures with affinity for each other. The long history of and the profound and extensive economic and cultural exchanges among the six countries have produced close people-to-people bonds among their people.

Naturally bonded together by the river, based on their historical traditions and realistic needs, the six countries are working closer than ever before to open up a new pathway to development, that is, the LMC, which has been launched not only for the purpose of building a river of peace and development, but also for pursuing the well-being of the people in the river basin.

China echoed Thailand when it first proposed to establish a cooperation mechanism among the six countries in 2012. In November 2014, the Chinese Premier further proposed at the 17th China-ASEAN Summit to "explore the establishment of a Lancang-Mekong dialogue and cooperative mechanism under the China-ASEAN '10 + 1' framework."

In November 2015, China and the Mekong countries held the First LMC Foreign Ministers' Meeting under the theme of "Shared River, Shared Future" in Jinghong, Xishuangbanna, Yunnan Province, China, at which all parties conducted in-depth discussions on strengthening the LMC, and reached a broad consensus on their cooperation.

In March 2016, the First LMC Leaders' Meeting was held in Sanya, Hainan Province, China, at which the LMC process was officially launched. In January 2018, the Second LMC Leaders' Meeting was held in Phnom Penh, Cambodia, marking the transition of the LMC from the incubation period to the growth period. In August 2020, the Third LMC Leaders' Meeting was held via video-conferencing, pushing the LMC into a period of comprehensive development and sending a positive signal of solidarity, cooperation, and common development among the six participating countries.

In December 2023, the Fourth LMC Leaders' Meeting was held via video link. The six countries will work in synergy to build a Lancang-Mekong community with a shared future, jointly advance the modernization, and drive LMC to a higher level.

In recent years, under the background of the intertwining pandemic and the changes of the century, the six countries have joined hands to overcome difficulties and made unremitting efforts to promote the continuous development of the LMC, strengthening it to achieve further prosperity. The LMC is continuously bearing fruit, and it has become an important part of the Belt and Road Initiative, as well as setting an example as the most potential experimental pioneer area and "foothold" for building a community with a shared future among the neighboring countries.

The Mekong River in Luang Prabang

The Mekong River in Phnom Penh

The "3 + 5 + X" cooperation framework Sets the Tone

Under the previously established "3 + 5" cooperation framework or the LMC, the cooperative areas have been constantly expanded to include the digital economy, environmental protection, health, customs, and youth, among others, on which a new "3 + 5 + X" cooperation framework took shape. It evidences continuous improvement of the LMC mechanism and the constant development of the multi-level cooperation pattern that is "guided by leaders and underpinned by all-round cooperation and broad participation."

The Tailor-Made "3 + 5 + X" Cooperation Framework as a Top-Level Design

In March 2016, the First LMC Leaders' Meeting was held. At the meeting, the six Lancang-Mekong countries jointly identified the three cooperation pillars which consist of political and security issues, economic and sustainable development, and social, cultural, and people-to-people exchanges, as well as the five key priority areas including connectivity, production capacity, cross-border economic cooperation, water resources, agriculture, and poverty reduction. In January 2018, the Second LMC Leaders' Meeting was held, during which the Phnom Penh Declaration of the Second LMC Leaders' Meeting was adopted, which proposed to actively expand the cooperation to new areas on the basis of consolidating the original framework, so as to form a new "3 + 5 + X" cooperation framework, under which cooperation regarding customs, health, youth, etc., will be expanded, and practical cooperation will be strengthened with strong support from all parties.

A Multi-dimensional Cooperation Platform That Operates Smoothly

The LMC Leaders' Meetings, the LMC Foreign Ministers' Meetings, the LMC Senior Officials' Meetings, and the LMC working group meetings work effectively with a clear division of labor among each other. A multi-dimensional cooperation platform composed of a joint working group, various cooperation centers, and non-governmental exchange mechanisms has been established and constantly improved.

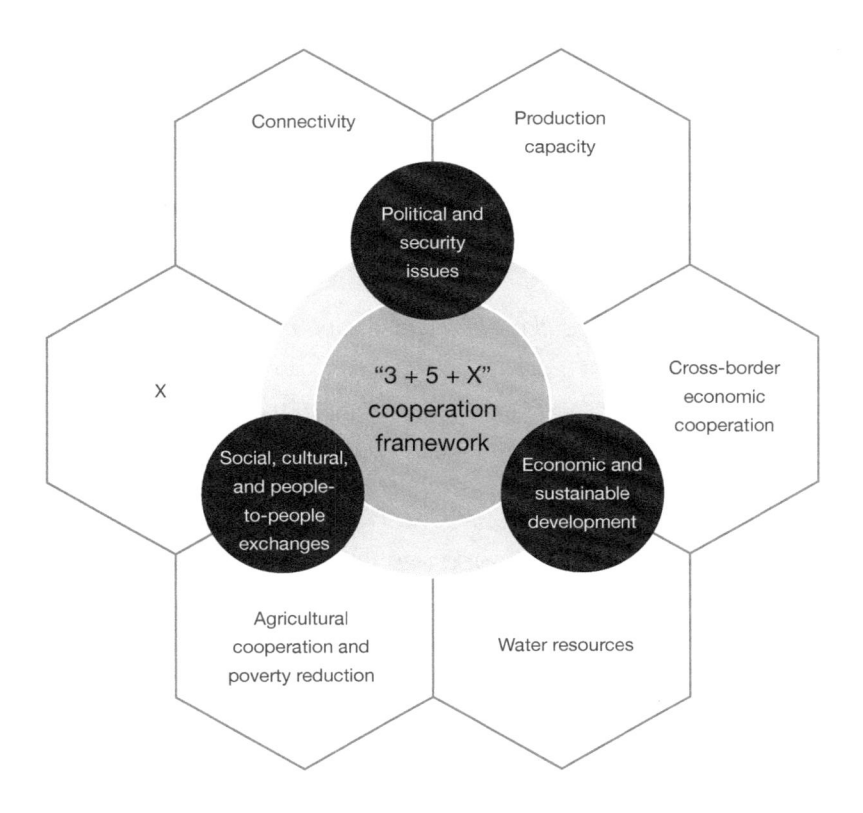

The "3 + 5 + X" LMC Framework

The cooperation mechanism

| Meetings of various levels

· Leaders' meetings

The LMC Leaders' Meetings are held every two years with the purpose of formulating strategic planning for the long-term development of the LMC.

· Foreign ministers' meetings

The LMC Foreign Ministers' Meetings are held annually to conduct collaborative policy planning and develop co-ordination strategies.

· Senior officials' meetings and work group meetings

The Senior Officials' Meetings and working group meetings are held several times a year as needed to discuss and implement cooperation in specific areas.

| A multi-dimensional cooperation platform

· The joint working group

The joint working group is mainly composed of officials and experts from the leading ministries and committees of specific areas from the six participating countries. The joint working group's meeting is held at least once a year to promote the sharing of information and also a full consultation among the related parties, which paves the way for the LMC Foreign Ministers' Meetings and the LMC Leaders' meetings.

· *Various cooperation centers*

Currently, various cooperation centers include the Lancang-Mekong Water Resources Cooperation Center, the Lancang-Mekong Environmental Cooperation Center, the Lancang-Mekong Agricultural Cooperation Center, the Lancang-Mekong Youth Exchange and Cooperation Center, the Lancang-Mekong Vocational Education Training Center, and the Global Center for Mekong Studies.

· *Non-governmental exchange mechanisms*

Non-governmental exchange mechanisms include the Lancang-Mekong Business Council, the Lancang-Mekong Sub-Regional Commodity Exposition, the Lancang-Mekong International Film Week, the Lancang-Mekong Tourist Cities Cooperation Alliance Conference, the Lancang-Mekong Vocational Education Alliance Forum, etc.

Six Countries Working Together for Shared Benefit

Since the launch of the LMC, the six participating countries have maintained close high-level exchanges, and their mutual trust in the political arena has been continuously strengthened. The diplomatic exchanges among the Heads of China and that of the five Mekong countries have set the tone for the overall friendly LMC, promoting effective bilateral relations among the participating countries, opening a new chapter in the building of a community with a shared future locally, bringing the awareness of a community with a shared future to take root and bear fruitful results, which benefits people from various countries.

Mutual Trust that Consolidates a Community with a Shared Future

Senior Official Meetings Set the Direction for the LMC

So far, high-level meetings have included four LMC Leaders' Meetings and eight LMC Foreign Ministers' Meetings.

» The First LMC Foreign Ministers' Meeting

On November 12, 2015, the First LMC Foreign Ministers' Meeting was held in Jinghong, Yunnan Province. At the meeting, the Concept Paper on the Framework of the LMC and the Joint Press Communiqué of the First LMC Foreign Ministers' Meeting were issued, and an agreement between foreign ministers of the six participating countries was reached on the targets, principles, key areas, mechanisms, and frameworks of the LMC. Arrangements were made for the First LMC Leaders' Meeting and the implementation of a list of "early harvest" projects, which were to be started as soon as possible.

» The First LMC Leaders' Meeting

On March 23, 2016, the First LMC Leaders' Meeting was held in Sanya, Hainan Province, China, and was attended by the Premier of the State Council of the People's Republic of China and the Heads of State/Government of the other five Mekong countries. The six parties unanimously agreed to jointly build a community with a shared future among the Lancang-Mekong countries and established the "3 + 5" cooperation framework. The meeting adopted the Sanya Declaration of the First LMC Leaders' Meeting and the Joint Statement on Production Capacity Cooperation among Lancang-Mekong Countries and approved the joint list of "early harvest" projects, which included 45 projects in connectivity, water resources, sanitation, and poverty reduction.

» The Second LMC Foreign Ministers' Meeting

On December 23, 2016, the Second LMC Foreign Ministers' Meeting was held in Siem Reap, Cambodia. The meeting focused on reviewing the progress of the implementation of the results of the First LMC Leaders' Meeting and reached a broad consensus in strengthening the construction of the LMC mechanism, deepening practical cooperation, and planning for future development. The meeting formulated three outcome documents, namely, the Joint Press Communiqué of the Second Lancang-Mekong Cooperation Foreign Ministers' Meeting, the Progress Report on the Implementation of Outcomes of the First LMC Leaders' Meeting, and the General Principles for the Establishment of Joint Working Groups regarding the LMC Priority Areas.

» The Third LMC Foreign Ministers' Meeting

On December 15, 2017, the Third LMC Foreign Ministers' Meeting was held in Dali, Yunnan Province, China. At the meeting, the Joint Press Communiqué of the Third LMC Foreign Ministers' Meeting was issued, the Five-Year Plan of Action on LMC (2018–2022) was approved and agreed to be submitted to the Second Leader's Meeting, a Hotline Information Platform for the LMC was established, the List of the Projects Supported by the LMC Special Fund of 2017 was announced, and the Matrix of Follow-Ups to the Outcomes of the First LMC Leaders' Meeting and the Second Foreign Ministers' Meeting was distributed.

» **The Second LMC Leaders' Meeting**

On January 10, 2018, the Second LMC Leaders' Meeting was held in Phnom Penh, Cambodia, and was attended by the leaders of the six countries. It was pointed out at the meeting that the participating countries should focus their cooperation on water resources, production capacities, agriculture, human resources, and medical and health care, so as to steer the LMC from a phase of nurturing to growth. The leaders of the six countries unanimously agreed to develop a "3 + 5 + X" cooperation framework so as to expand their cooperation on customs, health, and youth, among other areas. At the meeting, the Phnom Penh Declaration of the Second LMC Leaders' Meeting and the Five-Year Plan of Action on Lancang-Mekong Cooperation (2018–2022) were issued, and the List of the Second Batch of Projects agreed upon in the Second Leaders' Meeting and Reports of the six Joint Working Groups on the key priority areas were distributed.

» **The Fourth LMC Foreign Ministers' Meeting**

On December 17, 2018, the Fourth LMC Foreign Ministers' Meeting was held in Luang Prabang, Laos. At the meeting, the Joint Press Communiqué of the Fourth Foreign Ministers' Meeting was approved, and the Progress Report for the Year 2018 on Implementing the Five-Year Plan of Action on Lancang-Mekong Cooperation (2018–2022), the List of the Projects Supported by the LMC Special Fund of 2018, and a research report on the LMC Economic Development Zone composed of think tanks of the six countries were distributed. The anthem for the LMC was also released.

» *The Fifth LMC Foreign Ministers' Meeting*

On February 20, 2020, the Fifth LMC Foreign Ministers' Meeting was held in Vientiane, Laos. At the meeting, the Joint Press Communiqué of the Fifth LMC Foreign Ministers' Meeting was adopted, and the Progress Report for the Year 2019 on Implementing the Five-Year Plan of Action on Lancang-Mekong Cooperation (2018–2022), the List of the Projects Supported by LMC Special Fund of 2020, a progress report of the year 2018 on implementing the Projects Supported by the LMC Special Fund, and the Recommendations for Jointly Building the Lancang-Mekong Economic Development Belt were distributed.

» *The Third LMC Leaders' Meeting*

On August 24, 2020, the Third LMC leaders' meeting was held via video link. The six countries took stock of the LMC cooperation and mapped out a blueprint for future cooperation, which gave new momentum to each country's economic recovery, development, and prosperity after the epidemic. At the meeting, the Vientiane Declaration of the Third LMC Leaders' Meeting and the Co-chairs' Statement regarding Synergizing the LMC and the new land-sea corridor were issued.

» *The Sixth LMC Foreign Ministers' Meeting*

On June 8, 2021, the Sixth LMC Foreign Ministers' Meeting was held in Chongqing, China. At the meeting, the Joint Statement on Enhancing Sustainable Developmental Cooperation among the Lancang-Mekong Countries, the Initiative on Deepening Cooperation among Local Governments of the Lancang-Mekong Countries, the Joint Statement on Deepening Cooperation regarding Traditional Medicine within the Framework of the LMC initiative were approved, and research reports and materials such as the Progress Report for the Year 2020 on Implementing the Five-Year Plan of Action on Lancang-Mekong Cooperation (2018–2022), the Joint Research Report on Promoting Synergy between the Lancang-Mekong Economic Development Belt and the new land-sea corridor, the List of the Projects Supported by the LMC Special Fund of 2021, and the Hotline Information Platform for the LMC were distributed. The Chinese side also distributed the lists such as the List of Letter of Intent between Chinese Provinces and Cities and Local Governments of Mekong Countries, and the Initial Measures of the Chinese Government on Promoting Synergy between the Lancang-Mekong Economic Development Belt and the new land-sea corridor.

» *The Seventh LMC Foreign Ministers' Meeting*

On July 4, 2022, the Seventh LMC Foreign Ministers' Meeting was held in Bagan, Myanmar. At the meeting, a joint press communique and four joint statements on deepening customs-trade security and clearance facilitation, agricultural cooperation and food security guarantees, disaster management cooperation, and cultural exchanges and mutual learning among the different countries were issued, and the Progress Report for the Year 2021 on Implementing the Five-Year Plan of Action on Lancang-Mekong Cooperation (2018–2022) and the List of the Projects Supported by the LMC Special Fund for 2022 were released, which demonstrated the fruitful outcomes of the LMC with detailed data.

» *The Eighth LMC Foreign Ministers' Meeting*

On December 7, 2023, the Eighth LMC Foreign Ministers' Meeting was held in Beijing. Focusing on the theme of "Jointly Striving for Modernization and

Cultivating New Strength in Subregional Development," the meeting took stock of the progress of LMC, and out-planned for the key work in the next stage. At the meeting circulated the Progress Report for the Year 2022 on Implementing the Five-Year Plan of Action on Lancang-Mekong Cooperation (2018–2022) and the List of Projects Supported by the LMC Special Fund of 2023 were circulated.

» *The Fourth LMC Leaders' Meeting*

On December 25, 2023, the Fourth LMC Leaders' Meeting was held through video-conference. Focusing on the theme "Joining Hands on the Building of a Community of Shared Future and Modernization among the Lancang-Mekong Countries," the leaders took stock of the progress of LMC and jointly planned for the future of the LMC to strengthen cooperation, enhance mutual trust, and consolidate the partnership. The meeting adopted the Nay Pyi Taw Declaration of the Fourth LMC Leaders' Meeting, Five-Year Plan of Action on Lancang-Mekong Cooperation (2023–2027), and the Joint Initiatives on the LMC Innovation Corridor Development.

A New Chapter in Building a Neighborhood Community with a Shared Future

The six Lancang-Mekong countries have declared neighborliness and friendship on various bilateral and multilateral occasions, promoted practical cooperation, and put forward a number of cooperative proposals and measures. Through multilateral visits, the exchange of special envoys, annual meetings, and meetings on multilateral occasions, the six countries have established and developed strategic partnerships with each other. The China-Cambodia, China–Laos, China-Myanmar, China-Thailand, and China-Vietnam communities with a shared future have been successively fostered, and the awareness of a community with a shared future has been constantly deepened and solidified among the Lancang-Mekong countries.

» *China and Cambodia*

China and Cambodia have traditionally maintained a deeply-rooted friendship, and the occurrence of the top-level government officials' frequent mutual visits has yielded a high degree of political mutual trust and consensus between the two countries. In 2016, President Xi Jinping paid a state visit to Cambodia. In 2020, President Xi presented the "Medal of Friendship" to Queen Mother Monineath of Cambodia, which renewed the next chapter for the continued friendship between the two countries. In 2021, China celebrated the 100th anniversary of the founding of the Communist Party of China, while Cambodia celebrated the 70th anniversary of the founding of the Cambodian People's Party. The ruling parties of the two countries have served as the backbone of leading the two countries and their people to continue their friendship and deepen their cooperation. The year 2023 marked the 100th year of the late King Father Norodom Sihanouk's birth and the 65th anniversary of the establishment of diplomatic relations between Cambodia and China. Over the past few years, the relationship between China and Cambodia has continued to reach new levels, and fruitful results have been achieved in the construction of a China-Cambodia community with a shared future. The two countries have maintained increasingly closer cooperation in international and regional affairs, pragmatic economic and trade cooperation, and highly consistent national strategies, that is, the initiative to jointly construct the "Belt and Road" proposed by China is highly consistent with the national strategy of Cambodia, which has opened up new possibilities for mutually beneficial cooperation between the two countries. Additionally, new progress has been constantly made in practical cooperation regarding economics, infrastructure construction, etc., between the two countries.

» China and Laos

China and Laos have been friendly socialist neighbors, with common ideals and pursuits. The profound friendship between each other has remained constant. Sharing similar development philosophies, the two countries have always been moving forward at the forefront of building a community with a shared future for humankind. In April 2019, China and Laos signed the Action Plan on Building a China–Laos Community with a Shared Future. Since then, the two sides have worked together to form a new outlook for the relationship between the two ruling parties and the two countries. On this basis, in December 2022, the two countries issued the Joint Statement on Further Deepening the Building of a China–Laos Community with a Shared Future, which was targeted at the two countries to jointly build a high-standard, high-quality, and high-level China–Laos community with a shared future, and to demonstrate the positive efforts in and set a fine example for the building of a community with a shared future for humankind. China and Laos, who not only have developed harmonious political relations, but also have enjoyed a rapid increase in their economic and trade exchanges and connectivity, have been leading the way in the joint construction of the "Belt and Road," with their most remarkable achievement as the China–Laos Railway, which has become a landmark project that demonstrates the friendship between China and Laos and the efforts in the joint construction of the "Belt and Road."

» China and Myanmar

The "Paukphaw" friendship has grown stronger over time. Apart from such friendship that has a long history, China and Myanmar also enjoy ever-deepening mutual trust and close cooperation based on mutual respect. The two countries have been committed to strengthening their exchanges in state governance, and improving their top-level design regarding improving the relationship between the two countries, which have become an important part of their efforts in building a China-Myanmar community with a shared future. In 2020, the 70th anniversary of the establishment of diplomatic relations between China and Myanmar, Chinese leaders paid state visits to Myanmar, and a series of commemorative activities were carried out by the two sides. China is also Myanmar's largest trading partner and constitutes one of its most important sources of investment. Under the common concern and guidance of the leaders of the two countries, China and Myanmar are committed to building a high-quality "Belt and Road," and to promoting the economic and trade cooperation so that it can grow more comprehensively and deeply.

» *China and Thailand*

Thailand has been an active promoter of China-ASEAN relations. It took the lead in promoting strategic cooperation with China among other ASEAN countries, and it was also the first sponsor of the LMC. Top-level government officials from China and Thailand have maintained effective communications with each other and have joined hands to cope with the challenges brought about by the COVID-19 pandemic. Further cooperation on political issues and vaccines between the two countries has been continuously deepened. All of these represent a concrete manifestation of the profound friendship between the two countries, which is usually referred to as "China and Thailand are as close as one family." In 2022, the 10th anniversary of the establishment of a comprehensive strategic partnership between China and Thailand, the two sides signed the Joint Declaration of the People's Republic of China and the Kingdom of Thailand on Building a More Stable, Prosperous and Sustainable Community of a Shared Destiny, and the Joint Action Plan for Strategic Cooperation between the Government of the People's Republic of China and the Government of the Kingdom of Thailand (2022–2026), based on which the two sides deepened their coordinated promotion of their practical cooperation in various areas, and worked together to build a more stable, prosperous and sustainable China-Thailand community with a shared future.

» China and Vietnam

China and Vietnam are not only connected by famous mountains and great rivers, but also bonded by similar ethnic origins since ancient times. The two countries have formed a comprehensive strategic cooperative partnership, and their top-level government officials have maintained regular political communication and meetings in a flexible manner. The two countries have also maintained active cooperation in various multilateral forums of international organizations such as ASEAN and the United Nations, aiming to promote regional peace and stability. Moreover, Vietnam has been China's largest trading partner among other ASEAN countries.

China has remained Vietnam's largest trading partner for 16 consecutive years, and impressive growth has been achieved in economic and trade cooperation between the two countries. On November 1, 2022, China and Vietnam jointly issued the Joint Statement on Further Strengthening and Elevating the Comprehensive Strategic Cooperative Partnership between China and Vietnam, which aimed to further consolidate the traditional friendship, strengthen strategic communication, enhance political mutual trust, properly manage and control the differences, and promote comprehensive cooperation between the two countries, so as to promote the comprehensive strategic partnership between China and Vietnam in the new era to reach new heights. In December 2023, China and Vietnam reached the consensus to build a community with a shared future that carries strategic significance, benefiting the people of the two countries and making contributions to peace and development of the world.

» China and ASEAN

The relations between China and ASEAN have experienced constant improvement. On November 22, 2021, China and ASEAN held a Special Summit to Commemorate the 30th Anniversary of China-ASEAN Dialogue Relations and inaugurated a comprehensive strategic partnership. At the summit, President Xi

Jinping proposed jointly building a peaceful, safe and secure, prosperous, and beautiful and amicable home, opening a new chapter full of hope for friendly cooperation between the two sides. In 2022, in order to fully implement the consensus reached at the Special Summit and to establish a comprehensive strategic partnership oriented toward peace, security, prosperity, and sustainable development, China and ASEAN issued the Plan of Action on ASEAN-China Strategic Partnership (2022–2025), in which they jointly planned the cooperative vision of working together to build a peaceful, safe and secure, prosperous, and beautiful and amicable home in the local region, determined the focus and direction of cooperation for the next step, and continued to enrich the connotation of the comprehensive strategic partnership, working toward the goal to build a closer China-ASEAN community with a shared future.

Bonded by the comprehensive strategic partnership, the Lancang-Mekong countries have developed closer and more dependable relationships with each other. In the process of the LMC, friendships between Lancang and Mekong countries will continuously develop. The Lancang-Mekong community with a shared future will become the first of its kind in Southeast Asia.

A CR series EMU train runs on the railway.

Successful Completion of the "Five-Year Plan of Action"

In 2018, the Five-Year Plan of Action on the LMC (2018–2022) was officially declared at the Second LMC Leaders' Meeting. It is the first comprehensive cooperative plan developed by the Lancang-Mekong countries in the process of their close cooperation. Apart from formulating a working structure requiring each member country to submit an annual plan to the Foreign Ministers' Meeting and implement the progress report, it stipulated a clear code of conduct in terms of the fundamental principles, the institutional structure, practical cooperation, the supporting system, etc., drawing up an operational blueprint for the LMC.

According to the Five-Year Plan of Action, the years 2018 and 2019 are the foundation-laying stages, in which the emphasis is focused on strengthening sectorial cooperation planning and implementing small and medium-sized cooperative projects. The years 2020–2022 are the consolidation and expansion stage, in which the member countries further strengthen the cooperation in the five priority areas and explore new areas of cooperation that help respond to the development needs of the member countries, optimize the cooperation model, and gradually explore cooperation on large projects.

Year 2022 is the final year as stipulated in the Five-Year Plan of Anction. Since the implementation of the plan five years ago, planning in various areas has been basically completed, and new cooperative plans are being formulated. As a result of the plan, the economic and social development of the member countries have been effectively promoted, and the cooperation between and development of the Lancang-Mekong sub-regional countries has been greatly enhanced. The plan is of great significance to solidifying the LMC and building a community with a shared future for the Lancang-Mekong countries.

Pragmatism for Common Development

The LMC has always been conducted based on the principle of "putting development first, equal consultation, being pragmatic and efficient, and staying open and inclusive," during which mutual communication and cooperation have been strengthened, the construction of the LMC mechanism and platforms have been actively promoted, practical cooperation in various areas have been vigorously conducted, and major development projects have been advanced in an orderly manner. As a result, practical cooperation in the five priority areas has been steadily advancing, yielding fruitful results.

Employing the LMC as a Bulldozer Instead of a Talk Shop

At the very outset of the establishment of the LMC mechanism, China announced the establishment of a special fund for the LMC, promising to grant US$300 million to support small and medium-sized cooperative projects proposed by the Lancang-Mekong countries.

China has also provided preferential loans in RMB, preferential export buyer's credits, and special loans for establishing modes of cooperation regarding production capacities to support cooperative projects regarding infrastructure construction and production capacities in the Lancang-Mekong region. At present, more than RMB 1 billion has been granted from the LMC Special Fund to support 779 public projects for the six member countries, which has effectively improved the well-being of the people in the Lancang-Mekong sub-region and improved the economic and social development level in the region.

Through actively promoting cooperation on the "new land-sea corridor," the degree of connectivity among the six countries has been greatly enhanced. Since the China–Laos Railway commenced operations on December 3, 2021, as of December 2, 2023, a cumulative total of 24.2 million passengers and 29.1 million tons of cargo have been safely carried. The Golden Corridor has come to show its prominent effect of injecting new vitality into regional economic and social development. A large number of connectivity projects undertaken by Chinese enterprises have been completed one after another, injecting long-lasting impetus into an improved regional economy.

Based on the principle of "putting development first, equal consultation, being pragmatic and efficient, and staying open and inclusive," since the implementation of the LMC, frequent economic and trade exchanges have been maintained, the quality of cooperation on production capacity has reached a new level, the connotation of Lancang-Mekong cross-border economic cooperation has been continuously enriched, institutional cooperation on Lancang-Mekong water resources has reached new heights, and cooperation on poverty reduction has benefited thousands of households.

Opening Up New Areas and Embracing New Challenges

In addition to the continuously enriched connotation of cooperation in the five priority areas, the LMC has also been expanded to include several new areas, such as public health, the digital economy, technological innovation, environmental protection, and climate change.

In terms of cooperation on public health, in the early days of the COVID-19 outbreak, the six countries held a Foreign Ministers' Meeting with a focus on coordinating the actions of various parties to jointly fight against the epidemic. At the meeting, the delegates discussed various issues such as the establishment of a joint response mechanism for major public health emergencies, the provision of supplying materials and technical support to each other, strengthening cooperation in vaccine research and development, production, procurement, vaccination, supervision, and other areas, and setting up a special public health fund within the framework of the LMC Special Fund to promote beneficial cooperation.

The China–Laos Vientiane Saysettha Low-Carbon Demonstration Zone.
New energy vehicles were ready for shipment.

On April 29, 2022, the inauguration ceremony of the Vientiane Saysettha Low-Carbon Demonstration Zone jointly built by China and Laos was held via videoconferencing, opening a new chapter for the China–Laos cooperation to address climate change. The project was carried out in the Vientiane Saysettha Development Zone (SDZ), which has played a significant role in China–Laos cooperative efforts to address climate change within the framework of South-South cooperation. The SDZ project is bound to promote Vientiane as a good model of being a low-carbon and environmentally friendly city in Laos and even among Southeast Asian countries.

Common Destinies and Mutual Support Nurture Friendship

Over the years, China, Laos, Myanmar, and Thailand have conducted joint patrol and law enforcement operations on the Mekong River, guarding the river with perseverance and consistency.

The 100th China–Laos-Myanmar-Tai Mekong joint patrol and law enforcement operations

Data interpretations for the China–Laos-Myanmar-Thailand joint patrol and law enforcement on the Mekong River

Over the 12 years since 2011, the law enforcement departments of China, Laos, Myanmar, and Thailand have dispatched more than 20,000 law enforcement personnel and 843 boat patrols, and have also conducted 136 joint patrols and law enforcement operations on the Mekong River.

136

7

Over 200 joint operations, including water and land investigating and seizing and segmental patrols, have been carried out, and 7 joint actual combats have been conducted.

136.93

More than 36,000 drug cases have been solved, and 136.93 tons of drugs have been seized along the Mekong River and the border areas.

66/107

Among the cases addressed, 66 of human trafficking have been resolved, leading to the arrest of 107 suspects.

25

At present, law enforcement boats from various countries patrol the river for 25 days a month, with a police presence rate on the river over 80%, and a 100% police presence rate at crucial times. The cargo throughput of ports along the Mekong River has quadrupled, compared with the same figure 10 years ago, and the average annual growth rate of the number of tourists has remained over 20%.

200,000,000

As of the end of 2023, personnel from the law enforcement departments of China, Laos, Myanmar, and Thailand have visited tens of thousands of people who live in the river basin, and have provided production and living materials worth more than 10 million yuan to the people of the surrounding schools and villages. They have successfully rescued more than 200 merchant ships, avoiding a possible economic loss of nearly 200 million yuan, and have also won the admiration of people from all over the world.

The Joint Mekong River Patrol Law Enforcement Operations by China, Laos, Myanmar, Thailand and Safeguards the "Golden Waterway"

The Lancang-Mekong River is a "golden waterway." Apart from serving the purpose of transportation, it also promotes economic and trading opportunities among countries along the river and enhances cultural exchanges and political mutual trust among the countries on the banks of the river. However, due to the special geographical environment of this region, transportation on the Lancang-Mekong River can face prominent safety problems. Therefore, the trans-national maritime security cooperation among the countries in the sub-region is urgently needed.

On October 31, 2011, the Law Enforcement and Security Cooperation Conference of China, Laos, Myanmar, and Thailand-Mekong River Basin was held in Beijing, China. At the meeting, a broad consensus was reached, the Joint Statement of China, Laos, Myanmar, and Thailand on Law Enforcement and Security Cooperation in the Mekong River Basin was issued, a law enforcement and cooperative security mechanism among China, Laos, Myanmar, and Thailand for the Mekong River Basin was officially established, and the joint patrol and law enforcement operations in the Mekong River Basin were launched on the basis of equality, mutual benefit, and mutual respect.

The cooperation regarding joint patrol and law enforcement has brought peace and tranquility to the Lancang-Mekong River Basin and has laid a solid

Poster for the documentary *China and Cambodia Sharing Weal and Woe* during the pandemic

foundation for safe business and cultural exchanges among the people of all the countries.

The Six Countries Joined Hands to Dispel the Haze of the Epidemic

Right after the COVID-19 pandemic, Cambodia, Laos, and the other Mekong countries have actively supported China in fighting against it. China has also done everything possible to help the Mekong countries fight against the epidemic, including providing anti-epidemic materials such as testing reagents, masks, and protective clothing to the Mekong countries on several occasions, holding anti-epidemic exchange meetings, dispatching medical expert teams, and assisting in their construction of nucleic acid testing laboratories and temporary hospitals.

On March 23, 2020, a seven-member anti-epidemic medical expert team composed of Chinese experts set off from Nanning to Phnom Penh, Cambodia. It was the first anti-epidemic medical team sent by China to one of its neighboring countries and also the first among ASEAN countries. A documentary titled *China and Cambodia Sharing Weal and Woe* during the pandemic was co-shot by China and Cambodia, telling the stories of the two countries joining hands to fight against the epidemic.

Since then, medical expert teams have been dispatched from Yunnan and Guangxi provinces to Laos, Myanmar, and Cambodia at urgent times on more than one occasion to assist with the local epidemic prevention and control work. With the purpose of actively sharing their anti-epidemic experience, various hospitals in Yunnan and Guangxi have organized a number of special training and technical guidance meetings that have oriented medical institutions in the neighboring countries.

In 2021, the six Lancang-Mekong countries adopted the Joint Statement on Deepening Cooperation on regarding Traditional Medicine within the Framework of LMC, showing their unanimous support for the use of traditional medi-

The album entitled *Picture Book: The Lancang-Mekong Cooperation* was unveiled at the third Anniversary of LMC and the 2019 LMC Week Reception.

cine in regional epidemic prevention and control and in the development of public health in all member countries. In addition, China established a special fund for public health of the Lancang-Mekong countries, supporting projects related to epidemic monitoring, the prevention and control of cross-border infectious diseases, and other projects with the purpose of safeguarding the lives and health of the people from the six countries.

Affinity among the People Leads to State-to-State Friendship

Rivers connect the six countries together and bring about close bonds among the people. Under the principle of being people-oriented, the LMC has promoted personnel exchanges among the six countries and effectively enhanced friendships among the people. As a result, cultural development, tourism, education, health care, news media, etc., have been promoted, the "Lancang-Mekong awareness" has been actively cultivated, and a Lancang-Mekong culture featuring "equal treatment, sincerity, and a family-like atmosphere" has been developed.

The Annual "LMC Week"

On March 23, 2016, at the First LMC Leaders' Meeting, the LMC was officially launched. In 2018, at the Second LMC Leaders' Meeting, it was agreed upon to designate the week of March 23 as the "LMC Week," during which the Lancang-Mekong countries are encouraged to hold a series of wonderful activities such as youth exchanges, the LMC International Poster Design Competition, cultural performances, think tank forums, business summits, and TV Featured exhibitions, with the purpose of jointly celebrating the development of the LMC, while fully demonstrating the unique charm and fruitful results that have been obtained from it.

On March 22, 2019, the Ministry of Foreign Affairs of China held a reception celebrating the third anniversary of the LMC and the 2019 "LMC Week." At the meeting, Assistant Minister of Foreign Affairs Chen Xiaodong and the ambassadors of the five Mekong countries jointly released an album entitled *Picture Book: The Lancang-Mekong Cooperation* (published by Yunnan Education Publishing House), and student representatives from the six Lancang-Mekong countries sang the anthem for the LMC entitled *Lancang and Mekong, a River of Friendship*.

On March 23, 2020, the 2020 LMC Week Online & Yunnan Minzu University International Day was held at Yunnan Minzu University. More than 100 overseas students from five Mekong countries, 26 student representatives from 26 Yunnan indigenous ethnic groups, and Chinese students studying abroad in Thailand, Laos, and Myanmar met online to cheer each other up amid the fight against the outbreak of the pandemic.

In March 2021, Chinese Foreign Minister Wang Yi and the ambassadors of the five Mekong countries to China jointly attended the reception celebrating the fifth anniversary of the LMC and the LMC Week for 2021. A series of activities themed on people-to-people exchanges among the six countries have been successively held, such as the Lancang-Mekong Tourist Cities Cooperation Alliance Conference and the Lancang-Mekong Mayor Forum on Culture and Tourism, the Dialogue between Historic and Cultural Cities of Lancang-Mekong Countries, the 2021 Lancang-Mekong Adventure Large-Scale Domestic and Foreign Media Interview Campaign, the 2021 Lancang-Mekong TV Week, and the Lancang-Mekong Youth Online: Lancang-Mekong Regional Governance Workshop. Such activities have continuously enhanced the people-to-people bonds among the Lancang-Mekong countries.

In April 2022, the opening ceremony for the Yunnan 2022 LMC Week was held in Kunming. More than twenty Chinese central government departments and more than ten local provinces and cities held over eighty colorful activities, including youth exchanges, think tank forums, and film and television exhibitions, celebrating the sixth anniversary of the LMC with the five Mekong countries.

The LMC Week kicked off on March 23, 2023, in Kunming, Yunnan. A series of LMC activities were launched during the week, including eleven events which displayed the unique attraction and fruitful results of LMC, such as the 2023 Lancang-Mekong Youths Lijiang Challenge, a seminar themed "Overcoming the Epidemic and Revitalizing the Lancang-Mekong Community with a Shared Future," the Lancang-Mekong Youth Exchange, and the filming context titled "Green Lancang-Mekong Lights Up the Dream."

Links in Media Being a Significant Influence on Cultural Exchanges

The media is a window to enhance understanding, a link to deepen friendship, and a bridge to promote cooperation. Since the first LMC Media Summit in 2017, the *People's Daily* has become more closely connected with the mainstream media of other countries. Through media training courses and a series of joint interviews, their exchanges have been constantly enriched, and cooperation has become increasingly solidified.

From July 2 to 3, the 2018 LMC Media Summit was held in Vientiane, the capital of Laos. Forty media personages from the six Lancang-Mekong countries gathered together to conduct in-depth discussions and suggestions on further deepening media cooperation and promoting interpersonal communication and understanding.

From October 12 to 27, with the theme of "Drinking from the same river and sharing a future bond in the Lancang-Mekong River Basin," the 2020 Lancang-Mekong Tour and interview activity for Chinese and foreign media was successfully held. Afterward, some media also visited Yushu Tibetan Autonomous Prefecture in Qinghai Province, Changdu in Tibet Autonomous Region (Xizang), Diqing Tibetan Autonomous Prefecture in Yunnan Province, Dali Bai Autonomous Prefecture, Baoshan City, Kunming City, and other places where the Lancang-Mekong River flows.

On November 24, the 2020 Lancang-Mekong Cooperative Media Summit, hosted by the *People's Daily* and themed "Cooperating to Fight against the Epidemic and Revitalize the Economy," was held online. Representatives from the relevant departments, mainstream media, and economic and health sectors of the six Lancang-Mekong countries discussed and exchanged their views and shared moments of friendship with each other, thus injecting confidence and gathering strength to jointly fight against the epidemic and promote the recovery of the regional economy.

On December 28, 2022, the First Lancang-Mekong Media Joint Conference was held via video link in Nanning, Guangxi, China. The media from the Lancang-Mekong countries spoke freely about the theme of "media integration and connectivity to promote innovation and cooperation" and jointly discussed how to strengthen innovation and cooperation in this era of utilizing integrated media.

Youth Cooperation to Promote Development of the Lancang-Mekong Region

When the youth prosper, the Lancang-Mekong countries prosper. Cultivating the new generation is the future of LMC. China and the other five Mekong countries continue to explore new ways of cooperation. They have set up the Lancang-Mekong Youth Exchange and Cooperation Center and conducted various activities, including the Lancang-Mekong Youth Innovation and Entrepreneurship Training Camp, to enhance the friendship among the young people of the six Mekong countries. Through joint efforts, the six Lancang-Mekong countries have made youth cooperation which becomes a calling card for connectivity among different cultures.

Timeline of the Lancang-Mekong Youth Cooperation

— 2017 07.29

The opening ceremony of the First Lancang-Mekong Youth Innovation and Entrepreneurship Training Camp was held in Xining, Qinghai Province. The eight-day training camp was held on the basis of the "Lancang-Mekong Pact," namely the youth innovation design competition which was based on river basin governance and development, and it was jointly initiated by Fudan University, Guangxi University of Finance and Economics, and other universities.

— 2018 01.30

Youth Innovation Competition on Lancang-Mekong Regions Governance and Development took place at the National University of Laos. This is the first time that the competition has been held at a university outside China, making the first step of the rotation mechanism among the six Lancang-Mekong countries.

— 2019 01.23

The final of the Youth Innovation Competition on Lancang-Mekong Regions Governance and Development was successfully held in Phnom Penh, Cambodia. The event aimed to cultivate the global vision and international working ability of the young people in the six countries along the Lancang-Mekong River, promote cultural exchanges and youth diplomacy among the countries, improve cooperation regarding governance and sustainable development along the river, and also actively incubate youth innovation and entrepreneurial projects.

— 2019 05.18

In 2019, the Lancang-Mekong Youth Leaders Cultural Experience Camp was launched in Kunming, Yunnan Province. One hundred and four youth representatives from China, Cambodia, Laos, Myanmar, Vietnam, and Thailand participated in a one-week exchange activity to discuss the responsibilities of youth in the LMC.

— 2019 07.22

The opening ceremony of the Lancang-Mekong Youth Exchange and Cooperation Center was held at Fudan University. University representatives from the six countries jointly signed the Memorandum of Understanding on the Establishment of the Lancang-Mekong Youth Exchange and Cooperation Center, officially announcing the establishment of the center.

— 2021 12.06

The opening ceremony of the 2021 Lancang-Mekong Future Diplomat Cultivation Program and the High-Level Forum of Building a Sustainable Lancang-Mekong Region were held in Beijing. Outstanding university students from the six Lancang-Mekong countries who are committed to pursuing diplomatic careers in the future actively applied for this opportunity. Selected by the organizer, more than 100 formal students participated in the five-day training and seminars using online and off-line modes.

— *2022 05.26*

The 2022 Lancang-Mekong Youth Entrepreneurship Lecture was held online, then the two-day Lancang-Mekong Youth Entrepreneurship Exchange Camp finally came to an end.

— *2023 03.20*

The collaborative art project of the Lancang-Mekong Scroll Painting for Youth Cooperation was displayed at Fudan University. Student representatives from the six countries reviewed the whole process of scroll making, from design and painting to final completion. It is a demonstration of the fruitful achievements of the Lancang-Mekong youth exchanges and cooperation in the past seven years. By participating in the painting of the scroll, the students were also giving the advice to promote the development of youth exchanges and cooperation in the region to a higher level, with better effect, and in a wider field.

The Lancang-Mekong Friendship Has Strengthened over Time

The people of the Lancang-Mekong countries enjoy frequent bilateral and multilateral exchanges, stronger cooperation, closer relations, and also a sound atmosphere of friendly cooperation.

The number of participants in the LMC has expanded, and the enthusiasm of all parties has continued to increase. Many provinces in China have actively participated in the LMC. Many commercial and cultural exchange institutions have also seen great opportunities to participate in the LMC. So far, just considering China, nearly 50 central ministries and commissions, and nearly 20 provinces, autonomous regions, and municipalities, and many think tanks, universities, associations, enterprises and media have participated in the cooperative process.

China and the five Mekong countries have actively carried out cooperation in disaster management, established cooperative relations with Laos, Cambodia, and other countries in disaster prevention, mitigation, relief, and emergency rescue. They also have promoted cooperation in the field of disaster management to constantly achieve new progress and have ensured economic development and the improvement of livelihoods in all countries.

The people from the six Lancang-Mekong countries possess friendship and sincerity in abundance. The LMC has always adhered to the demand-oriented direction. The five Mekong countries are faced with the realistic task of eradicating poverty and strengthening their respective national governance capacities. The LMC has actively adapted itself to the developmental stages and national conditions of sub-regional countries, and continuously invested in education, health, women, and poverty reduction, which are most urgently needed by these countries. China and the other five Mekong countries have actively promoted practical cooperation in vocational education and students from the Lancang-Mekong countries have been arriving in China, which has trained a large number of practical talents in various fields for the five Mekong countries. Only the nine training bases in Yunnan have provided professional training to more than 40,000 cross-border migrant workers, which has greatly promoted the development of human resources in the Mekong countries.

Women's cooperation in the Lancang-Mekong countries has also made fruitful progress. On March 25, 2022, an exchange event, which marked the sixth anniversary of LMC, entitled "Uniting Women's Strengths to Achieve a Shared Future," was hosted by the Guangxi Women's Federation and held in Nanning. Liu Yongmei, the chairman of the Guangxi Women's Federation, said that since

2022 workshop on financial support system for natural disasters in Lancang-Mekong countries

the launch of LMC, the Guangxi Women's Federation has successfully held three times of "China-ASEAN Women's Forums" and two sessions for public benefit consisting of activities related to ethnic cultural performances, forming a mechanism of holding one forum or ethnic cultural performance every year and carrying out nine exchanges and visits. A comprehensive platform has been set up for high-level women exchanges, economic and trade cooperation, and general communication between China and the five Mekong countries. The China-ASEAN Women's Training Center has provided various trainings on poverty reduction and professional development to more than 200 women from the Mekong countries. Guangxi Women's Union has also established regular exchange mechanisms with five provincial-level women's federations and associations in Vietnam and Laos, setting up more than 120 "border women and children's homes" in eight border counties and districts of Guangxi, carrying out cross-border drug control and AIDS prevention cooperation projects, and conducting practical cooperation in agricultural planting, border trade, the prevention of AIDS and drug abuse, and combating human trafficking regarding women and children. Therefore, the Lancang-Mekong women's cooperation model, featuring information exchanges, resource sharing, and experience learning, has been established.

The key to regional development lies in the people. The six countries in the Lancang-Mekong region have already formulated a new five-year action plan to draw a blueprint for the next stage of the LMC. Building a more secure and stable, thriving and prosperous, happy and healthy Lancang-Mekong region, is what the people of the six countries are looking forward to. At this new stage, the Lancang-Mekong people's bond will reach a higher level.

"Uniting Women's Strengths to Achieve a Shared Future," a group photo at the 6th Anniversary Exchange of the Launch of LMC

Timeline of the LMC

2015

04.06 Beijing, China
1st LMC Senior Officials'Meeting was held in Beijing

07.23 Bangkok, Thailand
1st LMC Diplomatic Joint Working Group Meeting

08.21 Chiang Rai, Thailand
2nd LMC Senior Officials'Meeting

11.12 Jinghong, Yunnan, China
1st LMC Foreign Ministers'Meeting

2016

01.29 Kunming, Yunnan, China
2nd LMC Diplomatic Joint Working Group Meeting

02.23 Sanya, Hainan, China
– 3rd LMC Diplomatic Joint Working Group Meeting
02.24 3rd LMC Senior Officials'Meeting

03.23 Sanya, Hainan, China
1st LMC Leaders'Meeting

06.14 Kunming, Yunnan, China
1st LMC Joint Working Group Meeting on Connectivity and
Cooperation

06.23 Guilin, Guangxi, China
1st LMC Joint Working Group Meeting on Poverty Reduction
Cooperation

09.13	Nanning, Guangxi, China 1st LMC Joint Working Group Meeting on Production Capacity Cooperation
10.10 – 10.13	Yunnan, China 2nd Consultation on the Establishment of the Lancang-Mekong Comprehensive Law Enforcement & Security Cooperation Center (LM-LECC)
11.09 – 11.11	Beijing, China 4th LMC Joint Diplomatic Working Group Meeting to discuss the achievements of the 1st LMC Leaders'Meeting and next actions
12.22 – 12.23	Siem Reap, Cambodia 2nd LMC Foreign Ministers'Meeting, 4th LMC Senior Officials'Meeting, 5th LMC Working Group Meeting, and 1st LMC Diplomacy and Priority Areas Joint Working Group Meeting

2017 ■

02.27	Beijing, China 1st LMC Joint Working Group Meeting on Water Resources Cooperation
03	Laos Launch of LMC Laos Secretariat
03.10	Beijing, China Launch of LMC China Secretariat
03.31	Yunnan University, China 1st Anniversary & Review Seminar of LMC
06.08	Launch of Lancang-Mekong Water Resources Cooperation Center
06.13	Kunming, Yunnan, China 2nd Departmental Meeting of LMC Joint Working Group on Connectivity
06.23	Cambodia Launch of the LMC Cambodia Secretariat
07.10	"Blueberry Night" fellowship activities for LMC China Secretariat and embassies of the five Mekong countries
07.26	Kunming, Yunnan, China 1st LMC Joint Working Group Meeting on Cross-Border Economic Cooperation Siem Reap, Cambodia 2nd LMC Joint Working Group Meeting on Poverty Reduction

09.11 Nanning, Guangxi, China
1st Meeting of the Lancang-Mekong Countries Joint Working Group on Agricultural Cooperation

09.14 Nanning, Guangxi, China
2nd Meeting of the Lancang-Mekong Countries Joint Working Group on Production Capacity Cooperation

09.29 Dali, Yunnan, China
6th LMC Diplomatic Joint Working Group Meeting

12.15 Dali, Yunnan, China
3rd LMC Foreign Minsters'Meeting

2018

01.09 Phnom Penh, Cambodia
6th LMC Senior Officials'Meeting

01.10 January 10 Phnom Penh, Cambodia
2nd LMC Leaders'Meeting

03.01 Chiang Rai, Thailand
– 2nd LMC Joint Working Group on Water Resources
03.02 Cooperation & the International Seminar on Cross-Border Water Resources Cooperation

11.01 Kunming, Yunnan
1st Lancang-Mekong Water Resources Cooperation Forum

12.17 Luang Prabang, Laos
4th LMC Diplomatic Conference

2019

03 The Lancang-Mekong Environmental Cooperation Strategy (2018—2022) has been officially established

03.22 The Chinese Ministry of Foreign Affairs
The reception celebrating the 3rd Anniversary of the LMC & the "Lancang-Mekong Week"

04.02 Can Tho, Vietnam
– 3rd Meeting of the LMC Joint Working Group on Water
04.03 Resources Cooperation

06.04 Kunming, Yunnan, China
– 1st Special Meeting of the LMC Joint Working Group on Water
06.05 Resources Cooperation

06.12 Siem Reap, Cambodia
– 2nd Meeting of the LMC Joint Working Group on Agriculture
06.13 Cooperation

07.22 Fudan University, China
Opening Ceremony of the Lancang-Mekong Youth Exchange and Cooperation Center

08.10 Nong Khai, Thailand
The LMC Joint Working Group on Water Resources Cooperation 2nd Special Meeting of 2019

10.30 Kunming, Yunnan, China
The LMC Agricultural and Investment Cooperation Summit & Economic and Trade Fair

12.17 Beijing, China
1st LMC Water Resources Cooperation Ministerial Conference

2020

01.16 Chongqing, China
10th LMC Diplomatic Joint Working Group Meeting

02.20 Vientiane, Laos
5th LMC Foreign Ministers' Meeting

05.21 Videoconference: The LMC Joint Working Group on Water Resources Cooperation

07.30 Webinar: The Green Economic Development Belt in the Lancang-Mekong Basin—Roundtable Dialogue on Biodiversity and Sustainable Infrastructure

08.24 Videoconference: 3rd LMC Leaders' Meeting

09.24 2nd videoconference: The LMC Joint Working Group on Water Resources Cooperation

11.24 Videoconference: 4th Meeting of the LMC Joint Working Group on Poverty Reduction

12.29 Nanjing, Jiangsu, China
Seminar of the Lancang-Mekong Tourist Cities Cooperation Alliance

2021

03.23 Chinese Foreign Minister Wang Yi delivered a speech to commemorate the fifth anniversary of the LMC

03.31 The International Cooperation Forum on Traditional Chinese Medicine and the Fight against COVID-19

06.07 Chongqing, China
The Special Session of Foreign Ministers' Meeting commemorating the 30th anniversary of the establishment of China-ASEAN dialogue relations

06.08	Chongqing, China 6th LMC Foreign Ministers' Meeting
07.05	Beijing, China 1st Lancang-Mekong Fruit Festival
10.21	Chongqing, China Lancang-Mekong Tourist Cities Cooperation Alliance Conference & Mayors' Forum on Cultural Tourism
12.03	Opening ceremony of the China–Laos Railway Chinese and Laotian presidents attended the ceremony via video call
12.07	Webinar: 2nd LMC Water Resources Cooperation Forum
12.17	Beihai, Guangxi, China 1st LMC Local Government Cooperation Forum

2022 ■

01.27	Press Conference for the 2021 Top 10 News of China's Participation in the Lancang-Mekong Basin and Mekong Sub-region Cooperation
03.30	The China-ASEAN chamber of agricultural commerce launched the "Lancang-Mekong Agriculture Affection"—a series of activities to celebrate the Lancang-Mekong Week in 2022. It set up a column on the China-ASEAN Agricultural Resources website to publicize and demonstrate the positive impact and cooperative fruits of the LMC in Agriculture
04.07	Representatives of the five Mekong countries and Yunnan Province gathered at the Dianchi Lake, Kunming, to launch the Yunnan's 2022 Lancang-Mekong Week, and 14 activities were carried out successively
05.26	The 2022 Lancang-Mekong Youth Entrepreneurship Story Meeting was held online
05.31	The 2022 "Lancang-Mekong Week" Online Activity in the field of water resources was successfully held
06.13	China and Cambodia signed the 2022 LMC Special Fund Agreement to finance Cambodian Projects
06.30	In Nie'er and the National Anthem Cultural Party Education Base, Xishan District government of Kunming, the municipal government of Ruili city in Dehong Prefecture, together with the Yunnan Network, and the Yunnan Association for Industrial Development in Southeast Asia and South Asia, signed a memorandum of Joint Organization of the 2022 LMC China Rattan Open

07.04	In Pugan, Myanmar, Chinese State Councilor and Foreign Minister Wang Yi attended the 7th LMC Foreign Ministers' Meeting, which passed Five-Year Plan of Action on LMC (2023—2027)
07.22	Qinghai, China The "2022 Lancang-Mekong Week" and the Lancang-Mekong Regional Ecotourism Cooperation Forum
07.28	2nd Lancang-Mekong Fruit Festival was successfully held in Beijing. Opening ceremony of the China-Thailand Ecological Agricultural Industrial Park in Sichuan, which is a model for opening up and cooperation in modern agriculture in the Lancang-Mekong region
08.23	Gui'an District, Guizhou, China The China-ASEAN Education Exchange Week: The Seminar on Cross-Border E-Commerce Based Economic and Trade Development of Mekong Countries
08.24	Beijing Seminar on International Cooperation in Digital Economy among the Lancang-Mekong Countries
08.26	Yunnan, China Exchange named "Connecting the Lancang-Mekong Basin" was held to promote water resources cooperation
09.21	Kunming, China Online + Offline Forum: The Lancang-Mekong Poverty Reduction Cooperation and Agricultural Development
09.23	The Lancang River Basin Joint Media Gathering Activities themed at "Drinking from the Same River" The All-China Women's Federation held the opening ceremony of the 2022 "Lancang-Mekong Children's Nature Corner" at the China Children's Center
11.24	Yibin, Sichuan, China "A New Era of Win-Win Cooperation from the Same River"—the 2022 Sichuan-Chongqing-Mekong Countries Local Cooperation Forum
11.25	Beijing & Haikou, China Opening ceremony of and the keynote lecture on the "2022 Lancang-Mekong Seminar of Future Diplomats" (online and offline)
11.29	Taunggyi, Shan State, Myanmar Launch of the Myanmar Safety Channel Coordination Center, which is supported by the LMC Special Fund
12.08	Beijing, China The 2022 Lancang-Mekong Agricultural and Trade Cooperation Summit
12.19	Seminar on the Protection and Sustainable Utilization of Medicinal Resources in the Lancang-Mekong Region
12.28	Nanning, Guangxi, China 1st Lancang-Mekong Collaborative Media Conference

2023

03.01 Press Conference of 2022 Top 10 News about LMC was held in Lijiang, Yunnan

03.23 Opening ceremony of LMC Week and Series of Activities kicked off in Kunming, Yunnan
The Burmese Government celebrated the 7th anniversary of the LMC in Nay Pyi Taw by hosting a reception and achievements exhibition of Myanmar's projects supported by LMC Special Fund
Launching ceremony of the 2023 Thai Projects supported by the LMC Special Fund was held in Bangkok, Thailand

04.07 Chongqing LMC Week and International Design Competition of LMC was launched in Bishan District, Chongqing

04.20 The 2023 China (Zhejiang) Lancang-Mekong Cooperation and Development Forum was held on and off line in Hangzhou

05.20 LMC Dali Marathon

06.26 China and Laos signed the 2023 Lao projects supported by LMC Special Fund

06.27 LMC Media Summit took place in Beijing with the theme of "Promoting People-to-people Bonds and Striving for a Bright Future"

07.13 The 2023 Science, Technology, and Innovation Seminar on Potato Production in Lancang-Mekong Regions was organized in Beijing by the Institute of Agricultural Products Processing of Chinese Academy of Agricultural Sciences

08 Celebration of Metrology Cooperation in the 10th Anniversary of the "Belt and Road" Initiative and the 4th Lancang-Mekong Metrology Cooperation Seminar were held in Beijing

08.21 Lancang-Mekong International Video and Photography Week 2023 with the theme of "Shared River and Shining Images" was launched in Yushu Tibetan Autonomous Prefecture, Qinghai Province, the birthplace of the Lancang-Mekong River

08.28 2023 Lancang-Mekong Cooperation Mechanism Advanced Seminar on Cross-Border Tourism Cooperation was held in the Window for International Exchanges of Chongqing Culture & Tourism

09.10 The third Lancang-Mekong Water Resources Cooperation Forum was held in Beijing

11.03 The 10th Mekong-Lancang Cooperation Senior Officials' Meeting was held in Naypyidaw, Myanmar

11.08 "The Eminent Persons Forum on Lancang-Mekong Cooperation" organized by the Chinese People's Institute of Foreign Affairs was held in Beijing through video conference

11.11 The second Lancang-Mekong Security Cooperation Forum on the theme of "Global Security Initiatives and New Patterns of Security Governance in the Lancang-Mekong Basin" was held in Kunming, Yunnan Province

11.23 The Sichuan-Chongqing Region of China and Mekong Countries Sub-national Cooperation Forum 2023, themed "Together on a Path to Happiness, Nourished by The Shared River," was convened in Chongqing

11.25 2023 Lancang-Mekong Cooperation China Sepaktakraw Open concluded in Mangshi City, Dehong Dai and Jingpo Autonomous Prefecture, Yunnan Province

12.01 The 2023 Tengchong Scientists Forum themed on "Deepen International Scientific and Cultural Exchanges to Promote Science Innovation and Development in Lancang-Mekong Regions" opened in the city of Tengchong, Yunnan Province

12.02 The 2023 Buddhist Exchange Meeting in Lancang-Mekong Region was held in Xishuangbanna, Yunnan Province

12.07 2023 Lancang-Mekong Cooperation Summit on Agriculture, Agricultural Materials, Economy and Trade was held in Chengdu, Sichuan Province
The 8th LMC Foreign Ministers' Meeting was held in Beijing, themed on "Jointly Strive for Modernization and Cultivate New Strength in Subregional Development." The meeting took stock of the progress of LMC, mapped for the key work in the next stage, and made preparations and built up consensus for the fourth LMC Leaders' Meeting

12.11 – 12.15 2023 "Lancang River Journey" was held in Dali, Yunnan Province. The Lancang-Mekong Water Resources Cooperation Centre invited diplomatic envoys and journalists from Mekong river countries to have deeper understanding on China's contribution to ecological protection, river and lake management, and the role of reservoirs on the Lancang River in regulating flood and replenishing drought in the downstream countries

12.23 The fifth Lancang-Mekong International Film Week took place in Kunming, Yunnan Province. The Forum of Film Exchange and Cooperation of Lancang-Mekong countries was held and agreements on international cooperation projects were signed during the week

12.25 The fourth LMC Leaders' Meeting was held via video link, which issued the Five-Year Action Plan for Lancang-Mekong Cooperation (2023—2027)

Jointly Building a Prosperous Homeland along the Lancang-Mekong River

"I live at the start of the river, and you live at the end of it. There is unlimited affection between us because we drink from the same river together." The six countries are geographically and culturally connected, due to the location of the mighty Lancang-Mekong River. For thousands of years, people on both sides have lived by the river, bounding the six Lancang-Mekong countries together which led to cooperation and connectivity. Water-based resources are an important concern of these countries and a priority area for cooperation.

A River of Sweet Water Flows with the Initial Faith

We know each other far away, but we don't know how deep the river is. The LMC is born of the river, and water resources have been identified as one of the priority areas for the LMC. The challenges of water resources and the vision of common development constitute the strategic cornerstone of water resources cooperation among the six Lancang-Mekong countries.

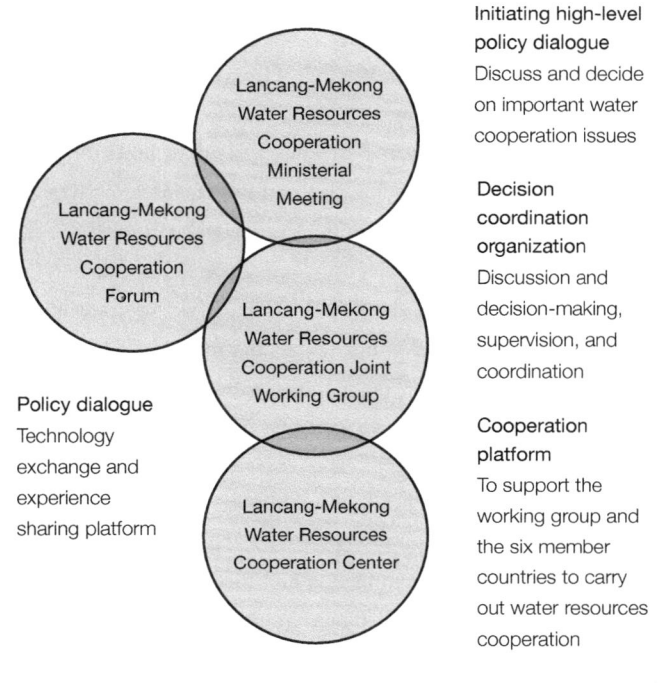

Initiating high-level policy dialogue
Discuss and decide on important water cooperation issues

Decision coordination organization
Discussion and decision-making, supervision, and coordination

Cooperation platform
To support the working group and the six member countries to carry out water resources cooperation

Policy dialogue
Technology exchange and experience sharing platform

Lancang-Mekong Water Resources Cooperation Ministerial Meeting

Lancang-Mekong Water Resources Cooperation Forum

Lancang-Mekong Water Resources Cooperation Joint Working Group

Lancang-Mekong Water Resources Cooperation Center

Lancang-Mekong water resources cooperation mechanism

Understanding the Top-Level Design

Water resources and diplomatic departments of the six countries have treated each other with sincerity and worked together to address the resource challenges of water resources in the basin. Lancang-Mekong water resources cooperation has brought tangible benefits to people along the basin. The water resources departments of the six countries have actively implemented the consensus reached by leaders, established a water resources cooperation mechanism featuring policy dialogue developed at the Ministerial Meeting, arranged technical exchanges at the Water Resources Cooperation Forum, organized and implemented joint working groups, and received comprehensive support from the Lancang-Mekong Water Resources Cooperation Center, thus achieving substantial progress in water resources cooperation.

In February 2017, the first meeting of the Lancang-Mekong Water Resources Cooperation Joint Working Group was held in Beijing, at which the Concept Paper of the Joint Working Group was adopted, marking the official establishment of the Lancang-Mekong Water Resources cooperation mechanism. In 2018, the Five-Year Action Plan on Lancang-Mekong water resources Cooperation (2018–2022) clearly set out the overall goals for Lancang-Mekong water resources cooperation for the forthcoming years.

In November 2018, the First Lancang-Mekong Water Resources Cooperation Forum was held in Kunming, Yunnan Province. Under the premise of achieving "Water Partnership Cooperation for Sustainable Development," the forum aims to create a platform for dialogue on water resources policies, technology exchanges, and the sharing of experiences. In December 2019, the First Ministerial Meeting for the Lancang-Mekong Water Resources Cooperation was held in Beijing. The Memorandum of Understanding was signed between the Secretariat of the Mekong River Commission and the Lancang-Mekong Water Resources Cooperation Center, which further promoted practical cooperation among the Lancang-Mekong countries.

In December 2021, the Second Lancang-Mekong Water Resources Cooperation Forum was successfully held via video. The ministers of water resources for the six countries, experts and scholars, and representatives of relevant international organizations and institutions had an in-depth exchange of views regarding water resources protection, climate change, rural water resources, and the improvement of people's livelihoods. They also shared their experiences and mapped out future cooperation. In March 2022, a special meeting for the Joint Working Group on Lancang-Mekong Water Resources Cooperation was held online. The joint working Group agreed that the LMC is the main mechanism for promoting sustainable utilization, protection, and management of water resources in the region. They will continue to deepen cooperation and make joint contributions to social development and the people's well-being in the region.

These high-level meetings and blueprint planning have provided strong political and policy guidance for water resources cooperation, played an active role in supporting and bridging the strengthening of technical exchanges, and also included aspects such as capacity construction, flood and drought disaster management, information exchange, joint research, and other aspects, and injected new impetus and made new contributions to building a community with a shared future for the Lancang-Mekong countries.

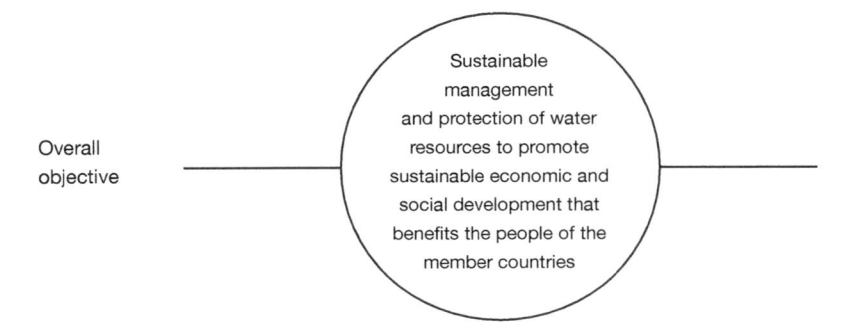

Overall objective — Sustainable management and protection of water resources to promote sustainable economic and social development that benefits the people of the member countries

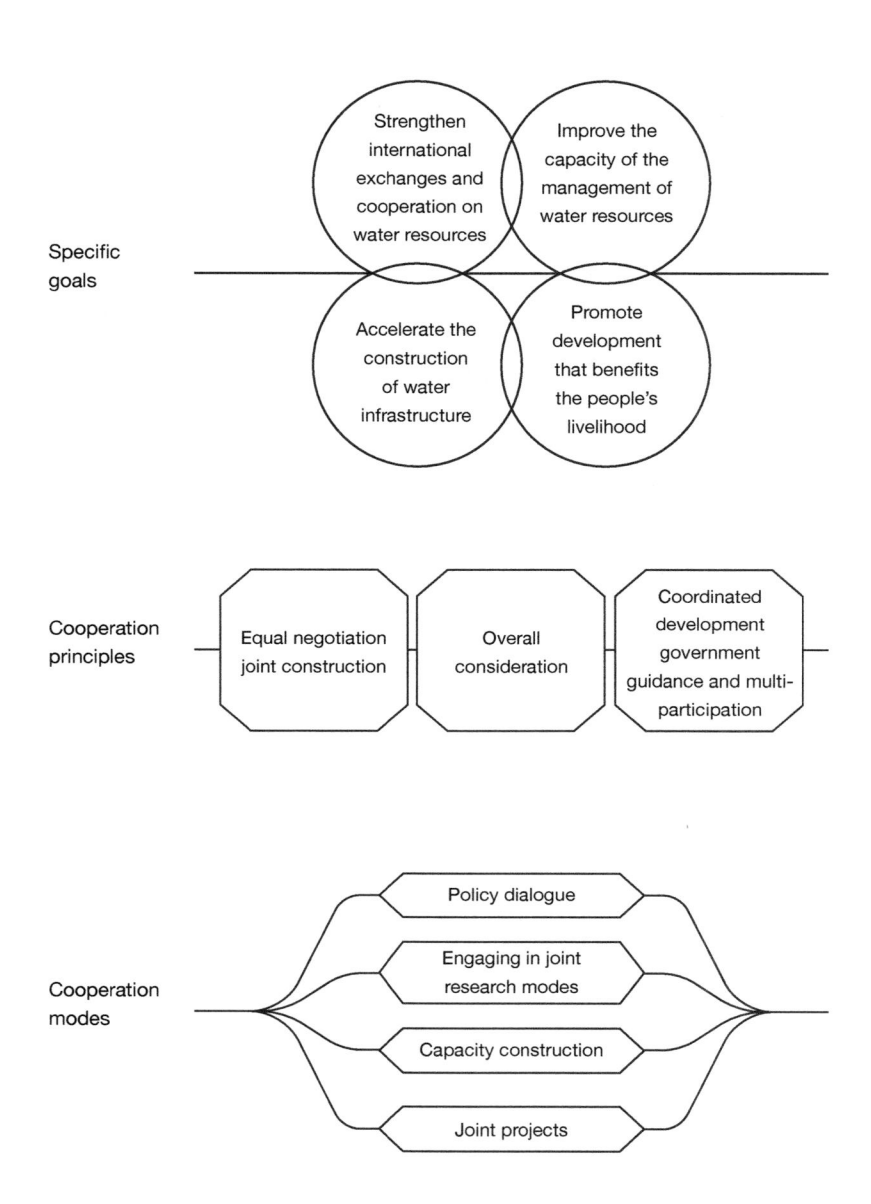

Five-Year Action Plan on Lancang-Mekong water resources cooperation (2018–2022)

February 2017

The concept paper of the Joint Working Group on Lancang-Mekong Water Resources Co-operation was created and adopted at its first meeting, marking the official establishment of the Lancang-Mekong water resources cooperation mechanism.

November 2018

The first Lancang-Mekong Water Resources Cooperation Forum is aimed at building a platform for water policy dialogue, technology exchanges, and experience sharing.

December 2019

The Secretariat of the Mekong River Commission and the Lancang-Mekong Water Resources Cooperation Center signed a memorandum of understanding at the first Ministerial Meeting on Lancang-Mekong Water Resources Cooperation, further advancing practical cooperation among the Lancang-Mekong countries.

September 2020

The second meeting of the Joint Working Group on Lancang-Mekong Water Resources Co-operation in 2020 deliberated and adopted the Memorandum of Understanding on China's Provision of Annual Hydrological Information on the Lancang-Mekong River to the other five member countries, under the Mechanism of the Joint Working Group for Lancang-Mekong Water Resources Cooperation.

December 2021

The second Lancang-Mekong Water Resources Cooperation Forum had an in-depth exchange of views on water resources protection, climate change, rural water conservancy, and the improvement of the people's livelihood, shared experiences, and mapped out future cooperation.

May 2022

The online event regarding water resources protection was organized during the Lancang-Mekong Week when participants had in-depth exchanges on joint addressing of the water resource challenges facing the sustainable development in the river basin. The website of Lancang-Mekong Water Resources Cooperation Information Sharing Platform was up and has continuously publicized annual hydrological data of the river, enhancing the six Lancang-Mekong countries' capacity to cope with floods and droughts.

2023

The third Lancang-Mekong Water Resources Cooperation Forum was held in Beijing to upgrade water resources collaboration under the framework of LMC.

Key meeting nodes of The Lancang-Mekong water resources cooperation

A New Story of Phongsaly

In the northernmost of Laos, located in the Nam Ou River Basin, there is a province called Phongsaly, which borders Yunnan, China. Surrounded by mountains, steep slopes, and deep valleys, the climate is like spring, namely rainy and sunny, all year round. Because more than 90% of its landscape consists of high mountainous areas, it is called the "Mountain City." The sea of clouds here is unpredictable, which gives it another very beautiful name—"The City of Clouds." The dangerous terrain and lack of transportation infrastructure have preserved the original ecology here, but also greatly hindered local economic development. At present, there are still many Phongsaly people who live in mountainous areas and have a very primitive lifestyle. Living here for a long time makes it difficult for the locals to improve their living standards, and a gradual degradation of the natural environment has occurred. However, with the progress of the Lancang-Mekong water resources cooperation, a new chapter is being written in Phongsaly.

In 2018, the Five-Year Action Plan on Lancang-Mekong Water Resources Cooperation (2018–2022) put forward "water resources protection and green development," and the cooperative topic, entitled "Integrated Small Watershed Management," provided the direction for the Lancang-Mekong water resources cooperation for the next five years. With the support of the LMC Special Fund, China–Laos water conservancy cooperation has reached a new level. In 2020, the LMC Special Fund (2020) provided assistance for the Demonstration Project on the Comprehensive Governance of Typical Watersheds in Lancang-Mekong (Phase I).

Yang'e Village in Mengsanpan County, Phongsaly, located at the Nanli River, was selected as the demonstration village of the first phase of the project, and the demonstration construction of the comprehensive management of the small watershed was carried out. The project follows the concept of green and sustainable development, draws on China's successful experience of green development in the comprehensive management of small river basins, and aligns with the needs of Laos' economic and social development. The project selects the Nanli River

Basin, a tributary of the Nam Ou River, which is in urgent need of improving residents' lives, promoting ecological and environmental protection, and also has a severe flooding problem which needs to be solved. The project carries out the comprehensive management demonstration of typical small river basins in the Lancang-Mekong countries and formulates an implementation plan for the comprehensive management of a small watershed. The pilot demonstration area of the project will establish a green development model by implementing comprehensive treatment projects, such as ecological environment restoration, the improvement of water sources for drinking water, the human living environment, the construction of ecological villages, soil erosion prevention and control, and consolidation and the improvement of the flood prevention system. Meanwhile, the smooth implementation of the project plays a positive role in improving the living environment of villagers in Yang'e Village, Laos, promoting sustainable development, ecological environment restoration, and other aspects, and also helps the China–Laos water resources cooperation enter into the "fast-paced lane" of development.

In 2021, on the 60th anniversary of the establishment of diplomatic relations between China and Laos, the Lancang-Mekong Countries Demonstration Project on the Comprehensive Management of Typical Small Watersheds (Phase II) project was launched, marking the "relay race" of Laos' small river basin construction demonstration, and also further strengthening China–Laos water resources cooperation.

On September 14, 2021, Chinese and Lao government representatives and project team staff jointly held the online commencement ceremony of the Comprehensive Governance Demonstration of Lancang-Mekong Countries Typical Small Watershed (Phase II) project in Phongsaly, Laos, and Beijing and Wuhan, China. In the second phase of the project, China and Laos will improve the demonstration efficiency from two aspects. The first is to focus on the "improvement of greenery and quality," namely paying more attention to green development and enhancing "project resilience" through "development." The second is to focus on "systematic" protection and governance.

As can be seen from the implementation of the "Demonstration Projects on Comprehensive Management of Typical Small Watersheds in the Lancang-Mekong Countries," Lancang-Mekong water resources cooperation has always been guided by a people-centered development philosophy, taking the improvement of people's well-being and comprehensive development as its starting point and goal, and also believing in the concept of being mutually beneficial and achieving win-win cooperation. It has effectively promoted the protection of water resources and the green and sustainable development of the economic and ecological environments in the small watersheds of the Mekong countries.

"Finally Got Clean Water!"

"There is no need to buy water anymore, because water safety is guaranteed. We said goodbye completely to the days when water was expensive and unsanitary!" said Sulapang, a resident of Hake Village, Mongway County, Luang Prabang, Laos.

The above is from a clean water project that was born from the LMC Special Fund, entitled "Lancang-Mekong Water Action Plan—a Demonstration of Rural Water Supply Security Technology," which solves the clean water problem for the villagers living in Hake Village. The project takes the "Safe Water Supply in Rural Areas," a key directive of water resources cooperation that was determined by the third meeting of the Lancang-Mekong Joint Working Group on Water Resources Cooperation, as the starting point, and adheres to the principles of having good-neighborly friendship, mutual trust and benefit, equal respect, and achieving win-win outcomes and shared development. According to the different types of water sources (surface water such as rivers and lakes, groundwater such as well water) and different water supply modes (small centralized water supplies and dispersed single household water supplies) in the Lancang-Mekong countries, it proposes systematic solutions to the typical problems of water supply security in rural areas, such as engineering water shortages and pollution-induced water shortages, and jointly carries out a technological demonstration of clean water security. A local technical system and regulatory framework for water supply in rural areas have been initially established, which has significantly improved the capacity of construction and management of rural water supply projects.

Luang Prabang is hot and rainy in summer. During summertime in the previous years, Surapong's family in Hake Village, Monway County, had to worry about clean drinking water.

"You can only buy water in buckets, which costs 6,000 kip (about RMB 5). When it's hot, you need more than 20 buckets a month." For the Surapong family, who make a living as fishermen at the Nam Ou River, drinking water is a big expense.

The LMC drinking Water Demonstration Project has become one of the most anticipated ventures for the local people. With the implementation of the drinking water project, entitled "Rural Water Supply Security Technology Demonstration in Lancang-Mekong Countries," the project team overcame numerous difficulties, conducted water supply surveys in the pilot areas, organized congregations of villagers to solicit their opinions, and effectively promoted the implementation of the project, which was praised by Laotian government departments and the people.

In February 2021, China and Laos overcame the impact of the pandemic and launched a project to renovate the old water intake point and pipeline and build a new one. A large centralized water purification plant was also built, and ten sets of small water purification equipment were installed for schools in seven villages around Hake Village and the reservoir area of the Nam Ou 2 Hydropower Station. Nowadays, the water purification system has been put into use in Hake Village, producing up to 15 tons of drinking water a day, which has finally solved the problem for the villagers.

"We are deeply moved by the real help which was provided from China," said Ben Tong, the head of Hake Village, "Our village is a new immigrant village and was planned and constructed by China Power Construction Corporation. Every family has a beautiful two-story stilted house, and is equipped with schools, clinics, village offices and markets. Now we have added drinking water areas and purification systems, and our days are getting sweeter!"

Similar stories are also being written in Cambodia. For a long time, the supply of drinking water in the rural areas of Cambodia has lagged behind. More than half of the farmers get water by digging wells. Some directly drink untreated water from rivers, lakes, streams, or even rainwater, which rarely meets the minimum sanitary standard. Therefore, drinking purified water has always been the desire of the villagers. The launch of the Lancang-Mekong Water Action Plan—Lancang-Mekong Countries Rural Water Supply Security Technology Demonstration Project made the villagers very happy.

At the beginning of 2020, due to the impact of COVID-19, the original work plan was disrupted and field research could not be carried out. In order to push forward the project smoothly, the project team quickly sought solutions, actively contacted their Cambodian partners, Chinese enterprises in Cambodia, and Cambodia's NGOs, and finally reached an agreement with Huaneng Lancang Hydropower Co., Ltd. and Sanghe II Hydropower Co., Ltd. Then they established a working group liaison to carry out in-depth discussions via videoconferencing and teleconferencing. The village of Srekol 1, a migrant village of Sanghe II hydropower station, was selected as the demonstration site. Each well, with its sources being located underground, provides drinking water for three households. However, due to the water sourcing problem, 2/3 of the wells do not produce water, so the villagers can only choose to buy the expensive bottled water or directly go to the Sanghe River near the village to get water. Therefore the safety of drinking water cannot be guaranteed. After selecting the demonstration site, the project team analyzed the existing water problems in this village, finally decided to start a rural centralized water supply project, and formulated the engineering technical scheme.

In October 2020, despite the twists and turns, the demonstration project was finally completed with joy, just like the autumn harvest. The centralized water supply project stores water through the use of highly located water buckets and then delivers water to households through a pipe network after it passes through a water purification system, so that the villagers can really enjoy the convenience of water usage. The decentralized water supply project pumps clean groundwater out of the ground through its mechanized hands, sending a stream of fresh water to the villagers and effectively solving water safety problems.

A series of livelihood projects have benefited the Lancang-Mekong region. Through the implementation of the Lancang-Mekong Water Action Plan—Lancang-Mekong National Rural Water Supply Security Technology Demonstration project, China has given full play to its advantages in technologies, intellectual property, and capital, including exporting its soft power in water conservancy technology and strengthening the "hard connectivity" of rural water supply infrastructure and the "soft connectivity" of policy, management, and technology systems. At the same time, it has also significantly improved the construction of rural water supply projects and the water supply safety assurance capacity of these countries, narrowed the regional development gap, and made rurally safe water supply cooperation reach a higher level. It has mainly aimed at improving the well-being of people in the Lancang-Mekong countries, achieving mutual benefit and win-win results, and promoting the healthy, stable, sustainable, and common economic and social development of the region.

The blueprint has been drawn and the project continues to be carried out. As Mr. Wang Yi said, the LMC on water resources should not be a "grand talking shop," but a "down-to-earth bulldozer." It has provided an inexhaustible driving force for the six countries to enhance their capacity in water governance and has laid a solid foundation for the region to meet water challenges and achieve sustainable economic and social development, thus helping water-based resources cooperation become the "flagship brand" of the LMC.

A River Accommodates People's Dreams with Glamorous Energy

The Abundance of Water Energy

"Seven Pearls" on the Banks of the Nam Ou River

The Nam Ou River, which originates from Jiangcheng, Yunnan, China, and borders Phongsary in northern Laos, is the largest section of the left bank of the Mekong River in Laos. It flows from north to south in a curvy and winding way and joins the Mekong River near Luang Prabang, which is a famous ancient capital and Buddhist center of Laos and is in the river basin. For a long time, due to the backwardness of electric power facilities, hotels and accommodations need to be equipped with diesel generators all year round, and the villagers have to store as much firewood as possible in their homes.

In order to ensure an adequate power supply, the Nam Ou River, with a total length of 475 kilometers, a watershed area of 25,600 square kilometers, and potentially excellent hydropower indicators, has become one of the water-energy resource bases promoted by the Laotian government. The Nam Ou River Basin Cascade Hydropower Project is an important part of Laos' strategic goal of building a "Southeast Asia battery," a key project implemented under the framework of the LMC, and the first overseas whole-basin hydropower development project built by Chinese enterprises. It is a model of China's hydropower technology and standards, which includes starting from planning and design to construction, operation, and equipment manufacturing, as well as the "going out" of the whole industrial chain.

Since the construction of the cascade hydropower project in the Nam Ou River Basin, China and Laos have paid a lot of attention to it. When completed, the project will guarantee 12% of the electricity supply in Laos, effectively promoting the upgrading and transmission interconnection of the power grid in northern Laos, which will not only satisfy the consumption of the local electricity market but also help Laos' electricity export and regional electricity integration process. The project has a total installed capacity of 1.272 million kilowatts and an average annual generating capacity of 5.017 billion kilowatt-hours, with a total investment of US$18.8 billion. The first phase of the project (Nam Ou 2, 5, and 6 stations) generated electricity in April 2016, and the second phase (Nam Ou 1, 3, 4, and 7 stations) started construction in 2016 and generated electricity for the first time in December 2019. With the production of the last cascade of the seven hydropower stations on the Nam Ou River, the project construction was completed in 2021, and the hydropower stations in the whole basin entered the system after a combined commissioning and operation period. After ten years of efforts, the seven power stations on the Nam Ou River are known as a string of dazzling "Seven Pearls."

Luang Prabang, a historic and cultural city, is now displaying some different views, compared with its usual charm, as the production of the hydropower station takes full effect. The roads are wider, the nights are more beautiful, and a number of new tourist attractions have sprung up. Sukan Benyong, deputy governor of Luang Prabang, said that the cascade hydropower project in the Nam Ou River Basin has boosted the economic development of the province, contributing to poverty reduction and community development.

In early March 2022, the former general secretary of the People's Revolutionary Party and the former president of Laos, Boungnang Vorachith, inspected the cascade hydropower project in the Nam Ou River Basin and highly valued its contribution to the development of the national economy. He praised the advanced management concepts, equipment and facilities performance, operational management quality, and efficiency. He also affirmed the major achievements of the localization aspects of the project and encouraged Laotion employees to work hard, hoping that the project would continue to provide clean energy, benefit the Laotion people, and convey the Laos-China friendship.

On April 6, 2023, when receiving the head of Lao Association of Chinese-invested Power Enterprises, Chalonsay Kommasit, the Deputy Prime Minister and

Minister of Foreign Affairs of Laos, pointed out that China and Laos are bonded by mountains and rivers, and have a long history of friendship, and that the two countries have made concerted efforts to promote practical cooperation to achieve remarkable results, which demonstrated the true nature of the bilateral relationship. He also said that China has long been providing support for the economic and social development of Laos, especially since CECC and other Chinese-invested power generation enterprises have made a lot of contributions to the economic and social development of Laos with their outstanding professionalism in the fields of electricity and infrastructure. For example, CECC has been developing in Laos for many years and has extensive influence locally. The most prominent case is the Nam Ou River Cascade Hydropower Project, the completion and full production of which plays a pivotal role in the northern part of Laos. The development and construction of the project, as well as its impetus to the local community, was obvious to all, providing a steady flow of high-quality and green electricity for the production and living as the stable operation of the China–Laos railway in the central and northern part of Laos. Chalonsay Kommasit hoped that

The Nam Ou River

the Chinese-invested power generation enterprises would continue to cooperate with the local government and the State Power Corporation to broaden channels, deepen diversified exchanges and collaboration, and jointly build a Lao-Chinese community of shared future.

The Promise of the Sesan River

The Mekong River winds its way from north to south into Cambodia and extends a tributary—the Sesan River in Stung Treng in the northeast of Cambodia. Above the Sesan River lies a 6,500-meter dam that straddles the vast plain. This is the first long dam in Asia and also the largest hydroelectric project in Cambodia— Lower Sesan 2 Hydropower Station.

Although Cambodia is rich in hydropower resources, it has long faced the problem of having an insufficient power supply and a dependence on imports due to suffering from an insufficient production capacity. The construction of the Lower Sesan 2 Hydropower Project has brought hope for alleviating this problem. With a total storage capacity of 2.72 billion cubic meters and a total installed capacity of 400,000 kilowatts, accounting for nearly 20% of Cambodia's total installed capacity, the Lower Sesan 2 Hydropower Station is powered by eight 50,000-kilowatt units made in China and can generate 1.97 billion kilo-watt-hours of electricity annually, which can supply electricity to about 3 million Cambodians each year.

On December 17, 2018, the Sesan River in Stung Treng, northwest of Cambodia, was integrated into the clear sky and shimmering water. The Lower Sesan 2 Hydropower Station was completed and officially put into operation for power generation.

At the ceremony for the completion and commissioning of the hydropower station, the former Cambodian Prime Minister Samdech Hun Sen said that the completion and commissioning of the hydropower station has further promoted the development of industry, agriculture, manufacturing, and tourism services in

Cambodia, and made important contributions to Cambodia's energy security, the people's livelihood and its economic outlook.

The largest hydropower project in Cambodia's history—the Lower Sesan 2 Hydropower Station, as a key project of the Belt and Road Initiative and Cambodia's energy development, has greatly improved the lives of the local people, provided strong energy support for Cambodia's economic development, and it has become a model for the LMC.

Water and electricity have a deep connection, which not only fast-tracks development in Cambodia, but also the affection in people's hearts. The construction of the hydropower station has been accompanied by the relocation of migrants. At present, all 840 households and 3,690 migrants who are affected by the water storage of the hydropower station, have moved into spacious, bright, safe, and beautiful new houses. The migrant villages in the reservoir area are being built into model villages to represent the friendship between China and Cambodia. Learning from China's poverty alleviation experience will help alleviate poverty in Cambodian rural areas. The friendship between the two peoples will be as deep and lasting as the waters of the Sesan River.

The villagers were very satisfied with their life after moving into the new village: "We moved to the immigrant village and never went back. The old village lacked some infrastructure, like electricity, roads, and it had tiny houses and farmlands. However, the new village has wide roads, tall houses, and new wells, and the power station has also set up a new power grid for the village. Now our life is much better than before!"

Dam 2 of the Sesan Hydropower Station

Adapting to Local Conditions—a New Plan for the Irrawaddy Delta

Agriculture is the pillar industry of Myanmar's national economy, accounting for about one-third of the country's total economic output, and 70% of the country's employment relies on agriculture. The Irrawaddy Delta accounts for almost half of the country's rice planting area and it is also the main grain-producing area of Myanmar. Agricultural production in the Irrawaddy Delta is of great significance to Myanmar's food security, economic development, and people's well-being. However, Myanmar's water-based infrastructure is inadequate, and its food security index lags behind that of the rest of the world. To stabilize food production and achieve economic growth, high requirements have been put forward for the support and guarantee of water conservation.

In 2018, under the framework of the LMC, the Ministry of Water Resources of China and the Ministry of Agriculture, Animal Husbandry and Irrigation of Myanmar reached a consensus, and the project, entitled the "Irrigation Development Plan for Major Grain-Producing Areas in Myanmar," was launched. The project aims to objectively analyze and evaluate the capacity and comprehensive management level of water-based infrastructure based on the development stage, characteristics, and patterns of Myanmar's economy and society. The project also aims to solve significant problems in the development, management, and protection of water-based resources in the delta region. Based on the improvement of the people's livelihood, the project has established developmental goals regarding irrigation as well. Focusing on the development of irrigation to improve agricultural production, it coordinates a flood control and disaster reduction system with the construction of supporting water supply facilities in both urban and rural areas, ensures food security, flood control security, and water supply security, and provides essential support for the safe, efficient, and sustainable development of the delta region.

With joint efforts from China and Myanmar, the project team has organized six different occasions for sending more than fifty technical experts to carry out on-site investigations and surveys in the Irrawaddy Delta. The team has also cooperated with the Myanmar Ministry of Agriculture, Animal Husbandry and Irrigation, the Ministry of Transport and Communication, the Ministry of Natural Resources and Environmental Protection, the Ministry of Energy and Mining, the National Bureau of Statistics and other ministries, as well as Yangon, Irrawaddy, and Bagu provinces, to solicit opinions and collect some additional information.

In 2019, the project was successfully completed, and the report, The Irrigation Development Plan for Major Grain-Producing Areas in Myanmar, was issued. It passed a technical consultation and was accepted by Myanmar. By introducing China's successful experience and the model of the "co-cultivation of rice and fish" according to local conditions, the new plan can effectively increase the irrigated area in the dry season, thus improving the planting structure, increasing agricultural output, promoting the export of agricultural products, and finally increasing farmers' income.

The irrigation water source project is also for the urban and rural water supply in the irrigated area, which is of great significance in improving its safe drinking water. At the same time, the ecological environment of the Irrawaddy Delta region was also taken into consideration during the construction of the project. By diverting water from the outer river to the internal rivers of polders in the middle and the upper parts of the delta, the ecological environment of the internal waters of polders can be improved. In the lower part of the delta, clean, fresh water is diverted from outside the saltwater intrusion line to improve the saltwater intru-

The Irrawaddy River

sion inside the irrigated area and improve the water-based ecological environment and human settlement environment. Finally, it can reduce flood losses, guarantee agricultural production, ensure flood control safety and food security of the irrigated areas in the delta region, and maintain the sustainable development of the economy and society.

The River Shines to Paint a Brand-New Eco-Picture

Green mountains will promote the well-being of humankind as long as human beings protect them.

Guard the Green Love

The scenery of two banks on the Nam Ou River in Laos, with the blue sky and green water, and full of vitality, is like a freshly unrolled painting. The Nam Ou River, stretching for 475 kilometers with its excellent waterflow rate, is the largest tributary within Laos and is located on the left bank of the Mekong River. It's surrounded by beautiful mountains and scenic landscapes. However, for a long time, inaccessible, desolate, and remote features were synonymous with the river. Building a beautiful home together is a commitment stemming from the LMC and China. From the rushing of the great river to the completion of the seven hydropower dams, from human inaccessibility to the chirping of birds and the fragrance of flowers, it has departed from desolation and remoteness to arrive at a living and working state that encompasses peace and contentment. Chinese builders have always upheld the concept of "green environmental protection and scientific development." With their continuous efforts, the mountains at the Nam

Ou River have become more magnificent, the water is clearer, and people's lives are becoming more enjoyable.

Respecting, conforming, and protecting nature are attitudes that are used to embrace nature and reflect our own sense of responsibility. The creative Chinese plan of having "one reservoir with seven dams and two phases of development" plays the linking and regulating role of cascade hydropower dams in the basin with a more scientific and reasonable design concept and also boasts the optimal utilization of water resources to minimize the resettlement of original residents, the loss of cultivated land, forestry inundation and the impact on the ecosystem as much as possible to maximize comprehensive benefits and achieve sustainable development.

The quietly flowing river has witnessed a "green miracle" during the construction of the hydropower dams. The sand and gravel crushing system is fully enclosed, advanced technology and equipment are used to remove dust and noise, and a spray system has been added to the conveyor belt throughout the entire process. In this way, the dust control rate reaches 98% or above. In the mountains, each hydropower station has set up a conservation zone for rare tree species, and vigorously implements the replanting of ecological forests. In the water, multiple animal habitat protection zones have been established upstream of the hub areas of each cascade hydropower dam, with various types of fish released in three dif-

Campsite of the Nam Ou 2 Hydropower Station

ferent periods throughout the year, and more than two million have multiplied and been released for nine consecutive years.

High ecological values bring benefits to people's well-being. At present, the 30 resettled villages by the unified planning and construction along the entire Nam Ou River have all been put into use, and the livelihood improvement project focusing on environmental protection and efficiency has also been fully launched, bringing new life to more than 11,000 villagers. With the opening of the 93-kilometer access road built alongside the seven dams, the occurrence of having nine villages along the line and four villages near the power station without having access to land transportation has changed. Export channels for jackfruit, bananas, rubber, amomum, sugar cane, cattle and sheep, and wild agricultural products in the villages, have also become completely unrestricted.

Farewell to the Nam Ou River, gazing back with a contemplative look, the lush greenery, the mountains are full of hope, and forming a deep attachment to the water …

A photo of the Hake resettlement village near the Nam Ou 2 Hydropower Station in Laos

The children from the resettlement village near the Nam Ou River in Laos

Protecting Fish Stocks

The Lancang-Mekong River has bred an abundant ecosystem of freshwater fish, with more than 1,700 species of fish, second only to the Amazon River in terms of fish diversity among the world's great rivers. The World Wildlife Fund has identified the Lancang-Mekong River as one of the world's most important freshwater fish ecological areas.

Fish stocks in the basin are vital to the livelihoods of millions of residents living in the area. The LMC places great importance on the protection of endangered aquatic wildlife and the conservation of aquatic biological resources, as well as the sustainable development of fisheries, to ensure the synchronous improvement of ecological, economic, and social benefits within the Lancang-Mekong River.

There are 34 species of fish that migrate long distances in the Sesan River. In order to minimize the impact of hydropower projects on the river's ecological environment, meet the needs of migratory fish as much as possible, and maintain the ecological diversity of regional fish, the Lower Sesan 2 Hydropower Station took the initiative to invest about US$1.5 million to build bionic fishways on the right bank of the dam even though the project's agreement and the Cambodian government did not require the construction of a fish passage, establishing a good

The fishway project on the Sesan River

image in regard to the Chinese companies' commitment to environmental protection and corporate responsibility. Compared with the concrete fishway, the fish passage resembles the natural river, maintaining continuity and integrity between upstream and downstream locations. It provides a diverse aquatic environment which is suitable for the growth of plankton with its wide section and large migratory space, and the abundant fish bait is conducive to protecting the diversity of biological species.

As the fishway engineering staff said, "The fish passages can be better integrated into the surrounding environment, just like a small river that originally existed here, and it is the way for fish to go home."

The story of releasing fish to protect the water and guarding the Lancang-Mekong River continues between China and Laos.

"Ready, one, two, three, let it go!" Fifty thousand lively small fish, including grass carp, silver carp, and tilapia, poured out and rushed into the tailwater channel of the Nam Lik 1-2 Hydropower Project. In the water, the river grass is swaying, and the fish and shrimps are playing, which are accompanied by the cheers of the crowd as this shoal of small fish swims into the distance and begins their journey of growth.

After the LMC Foreign Ministers' Meeting listed water resource cooperation as one of the five priorities of the LMC for the first time, the agricultural department of Xishuangbanna Dai Autonomous Prefecture and Luang Namtha Province of Laos signed an agreement on fishery protection under the LMC framework, thus opening a new chapter in the protection of trans-boundary fishery resources in the Lancang-Mekong River.

The fishery department of Xishuangbanna Prefecture has carried out multi-level and all-round cooperation with the Office of Natural Resources and Environment of Luang Namtha Province, and has provided aquaculture technology training for technical personnels of the Lao government and villagers by inviting attendants. It has also donated fish seeds villagers in the five counties under the jurisdiction of Luang Namtha Province, including Long, Nale, Namtha, Sing, and Viengphoukha, to help them breed indigenous fish species from the Lancang-Mekong River, aiming to reduce the catch of natural fish.

The Yangtze River Basin fishery administration supervision and administration office, under the Ministry of Agriculture and Rural Affairs of China, Yunnan's Provincial Department of Agriculture and Rural Affairs, the Government of Xishuangbanna Prefecture, and the Office of Natural Resources and Environment of Luang Namtha Province jointly launched the 2022 Synchronous Propagation and Release Program along the Lancang-Mekong River between China and Laos as well as the Joint Law Enforcement Operation of the Lancang-Mekong River between Laos and China on November 10, 2022. This is the eighth consecutive year that China and Laos have jointly carried out fishery law enforcement operations and aquatic species propagation and release activities in the Lancang-Mekong River under the framework of the LMC. Positive contributions have been made to the protection of the ecological resources, the conservation of aquatic resources, and the sustainable development of fisheries in the Lancang-Mekong River.

"The great river reflects the evening glow, thousands of miles run through countless homes; hand in hand to protect the ecology, crossing borders to chase the waves; enhancing reproduction and release, fish grow fat and shrimp thrive; the Lancang-Mekong is my home, together we care for her." The singing of the Chinese and Laotian echoes on the Lancang-Mekong River, highlighting the joint efforts of the two countries in protecting cross-border fishery resources under the LMC. The people of China and Laos share the vision of a beautiful future for the Lancang-Mekong River with "unobstructed rivers, clear water, green banks that promote natural ecosystems and safety."

The Nuozhadu Hydropower Station, located at the junction of Simao District and Lancang County in Pu'er City, Yunnan Province, is the fifth hydropower station in the "two reservoirs and eight hydropower stations" cascade hydropower development program that is situated on the lower reaches of the Lancang River. It is a large-scale major project and the permanent main hydraulic structure is a first-class building. The reservoir has a total capacity of 23.703 billion cubic meters, an adjusted storage capacity of 11.335 billion cubic meters, and a normal water storage level of 812 meters, making it the largest of its kind in Asia and the third largest in the world.

At the Nuozhadu Hydropwer Station, the fish hatching project involves six rare species that are found in the Lancang River. After continuous efforts, experts have successfully bred four of these species in large numbers and releasing activities are held every year. The construction of the reservoir is often accompanied by controversies over its impact on the local ecology. Before building a series of reservoirs on the Lancang River, engineers paid special attention to the protection of local biodiversity. Among the various options, the endangered flora and fauna were relocated to safer areas, which not only promotes economic and social development and meets the demand for irrigation and power generation, but also minimizes the impact on the ecosystem.

The Nuozhadu Hydropower Station has invested heavily in ecological environmental protection. The station features the "Two Stations and One Park" initiative—consisting of a rare animal rescue station, a rare fish propagation station, and a rare plant protection garden—that helps preserve the genes of endangered species and protects these scarce resources. In building a power station while protecting the ecology, "Two Stations and One Park" initiative presents a harmonious coexistence between humans and nature. This fact refutes rumors and fallacies such as "the development of cascade power stations on the Lancang River destroys the ecology," and demonstrates China's sincerity and efforts in protecting animals and plants during the developmental process of the Lancang-Mekong River hydropower stations.

The six countries of the Lancang-Mekong River have penned together, through deep friendships the harmony between human and water, depicting the beautiful Lancang-Mekong River with ecological brushes. This effort has effectively supported and ensured the stability of the Lancang-Mekong River ecosystem, while making new contributions to the well-being of the people in the region.

People releasing fish

Local Laotian people attending the stocking and release activity along the Lancang River

Nuozhadu Hydopower Station

The Northward Migration and Return Journey of Elephant Herd in Yunnan

"The construction of China's ecological civilization has achieved remarkable success. Recently, the northward and return journey of Yunnan elephants herd has shown us a specific achievement in China's wildlife protection." Chinese President Xi Jinping delivered a keynote speech via video link at the Leaders' Summit of the Fifteenth Conference of the Parties (COP 15) to the Convention on Biological Diversity (CBD) held in Kunming Yunnan Province on the afternoon of October 12, 2021. He specifically mentioned the wild Asian elephants in Yunnan. The journey of guardianship, spanning over 1,300 kilometers, has refreshed people's understanding of the Asian elephant population and prompted many people to start thinking about how to coexist harmoniously with wild Asian elephant herds.

Seventeen Asian elephants intruded into people's lives on a mountain adjacent to Yuanjiang County, Yuxi City and Mojiang County, Pu'er City on April 16, 2021. The Yuanjiang River is at a suitable intersection for the habitat of Asian elephants and the general habitats. The sudden arrival and leisurely northward migration of such a group of gigantic creatures disrupted the peaceful lives of the people.

This group is called the "Short Trunks," and they have crossed over half of Yunnan, embarking on an unprecedented and extraordinary journey.

The Short Trunks, a wild Asian elephant herd, were marching across the Yuanjiang Bridge on Aug. 8, 2021.

In order to ensure the safety of both humans and elephants, commands at various levels have been urgently established in Yunnan Province to start real-time monitoring and early warnings of elephant groups, and people who are within the activity range of the wandering elephants need to be ready to evacuate at any time. Respect, concessions, and protection have always been the keywords in the process of interacting with a herd of elephants. In Yuxi, when the elephants ate crops, the villagers said, "It's okay for elephants to be greedy. If they want to eat, they can eat. Our crops can be planted again next year, but if the elephants are hurt, they will be gone." In Honghe, in order not to disturb the herd, people expressed their love for Asian elephants through various ways such as pasting slogans of an auspicious "elephant," sending blessings of harmony between humans and elephants, drawing "elephant" symbols, and singing and dancing to send messages of auspiciousness, instead of holding celebrations or lighting fireworks to pray for blessings during traditional festivals. Such examples are too numerous to enumerate. The touching scenes, vivid pictures, and intricate details of the Asian elephants' journey from the south to the north fully demonstrate the spirit of loving and protecting them among the public and they have become a vivid epitome of promoting harmonious coexistence between humans and nature in China.

The Short Trunks, though only roaming in Yunnan, have made a global impact and have become a fascinating Chinese story shared with the world. A picture of the young family members of the elephants sleeping soundly in the forest because of fatigue was captured by a drone. In a flash, it was spread all over the world. The achievements of China's wildlife conservation efforts have been widely publicized in a vivid and warm manner, gaining praise from significant realms of global media.

The Japanese media made a special program that extensively showcased the fantastic journey of the elephant herd and also made a favorable comment that "The Xishuangbanna Nature Reserve is different from wildlife parks in that it does not have barriers to contain animals. The elephant families will not be stopped when they go out and the Chinese government's care for migrating elephants is impressive." The overall improvement of China's ecological environment, the government and people's love for wildlife, the rapid response of relevant departments in this instance and the protection measures taken throughout the process, to a considerable extent, have offset some of the foreign media's false and negative opinions on China. The incredible journey of the "Short Trunks" has become a vivid example of China's efforts to promote the coexistence between humans and nature, and the harmony between humans and animals in China. It has also demonstrated a compassionate and beautiful "Chinese model" to global wildlife conservation work.

The Short Trunks rested in the forest in the new Laijia Village, Xiyang Township, Jinning District, Kunming City on June 6, 2021.

Fruitful and Unique as It Is, Forget Not Its Primary Aspiration

For a tree to grow tall, its roots must go deep; for a river to flow well, its source must be far away.

Shared River and Shared Data

Only in Jinghong, when looking to the north, people can understand that there is a large river called the Lancang River, and it is called the Mekong River for its south section. At Jinghong Port, clouds are reflected in the Lancang River and further south at the junction of China, Laos, and Myanmar, is the Guanlei Port where the Lancang River turns into the Mekong River. Although the names are different, the river keeps flowing, and people along the river still share the same destiny.

At the Third LMC Leaders' Meeting in 2020, the Chinese Premier proposed that "China will share the year-round hydrological data from the Lancang River with the countries along the Mekong River from this year forward," which has accelerated the process of sharing hydrological information among the six countries. The Memorandum of Understanding on China's Provision of Annual Hydrological Information on the Lancang-Mekong River to the other five member contries, under the Mechanism of the Joint Working Group for Lancang-Mekong Water Resoures Cooperation was officially signed on September 24, 2020, and on October 22. An agreement between the Ministry of Water Resources of the People's Republic of China and the Mekong River Commission on China's Provision of Year-Round Hydrological Information on the Lancang River to the Secretariat of the Mekong River Commission was signed at the 24th Dialogue Meeting of the MRC Joint Committee and Mekong River Commission. In accordance with the memorandum and the agreement, China will provide the five Mekong countries and the Mekong River Commission with the year-round hydrological data of the two international hydrological stations in Yunjinghong and Man'an along the Lancang River starting from November 1, 2020.

The opening ceremony of the website of the Lancang-Mekong Water Resources Cooperative Information Sharing Platform, initiated by China, was held in Beijing on November 30, 2020. The establishment of the website, actively sharing relevant information, comprehensively and systematically displaying cooperative achievements in water resources for the Lancang-Mekong region, and objectively and accurately sharing the knowledge of transboundary rivers are not only important measures adopted by China to implement the consensus of leaders from the six countries, but also demonstrate China's firm determination to promote the LMC and enhance the partnership on water resources cooperation. Water management is a contemporary achievement that will benefit future generations. Strengthening data, information, knowledge, experience, and sharing technology in the field of water resources among the six countries in the Lancang-Mekong region and building a Lancang-Mekong water resources information-sharing platform, are of great significance in promoting the security of water resources in the basin and sustainable economic and social development in all countries involved.

In addition, with the support of the LMC, the launch of the Pilot Project of Hydrological Observation and Data Transmission in Laos and Cambodia has helped to enhance the monitoring capabilities and personnel techniques of hydrological data collection and transmission in the countries along the river and

Jinghong Hydropower Station

provides technical support for flood control, disaster reduction, and water resource utilization in the region. Currently, the achievements of the project have been widely applied in Laos and Cambodia. The completed system can quickly transmit hydrological and meteorological information and quickly collect, inspect, correct, and automatically standardize this information, which can be automatically forwarded to targeted locations, providing accurate and real-time rain information for flood control commands at all levels in the basin countries, offering scientific evidence for the rational use of water resources, flood control scheduling, emergency rescues, and disaster relief operations, while serving local, national economic development, flood and drought control, and engineering management operations.

You Are a Part of Me, and I Am a Part of You

The Lancang-Mekong River is an important support for the economic and social development of the countries in the basin. However, the rainy and dry seasons are clearly distinguishable. Water shortages are common during the dry season. In recent years, under the influence of global climate change, droughts in the basin have occurred more frequently, intensified, and widespread, affecting people's production and livelihood and bringing adverse impacts on the ecological environment. For example, the precipitation and natural runoff in the Lancang River Basin were about 30% less than usual from June to October 2010. Rainfall at hydrological stations in Chiang Saen, Luang Prabang, and Nong Khai, the mainstream of the Mekong River, decreased by 40%, 50%, and 20%, respectively, compared with the same period of previous years. Nevertheless, drought, as a natural phenomenon, can be alleviated through the use of reservoirs, which can reduce peaks during the flood season, increase the discharge flow during the dry season, and jointly regulate tributary reservoirs.

At the end of 2015, the countries in the Lancang-Mekong River Basin suffered from drought of varying degrees due to the strong El Niño phenomenon, and the water level of the Mekong River dropped to its lowest point in almost

90 years. However, data shows that, despite a 20% decrease in water inflow to the basin and an inflow rate of only about 500 cubic meters per second since 2016, the discharge of cascade hydropower stations on the Lancang River has reached about 1,000 cubic meters per second, and a total of 2.7 billion cubic meters of water has been replenished downstream, a 94% increase over natural water inflow, which has effectively improved the water supply in the downstream areas during the dry season, and the effects of reducing the high flow and replenishing the low flow is obvious.

To address concerns from countries in the basin, China has made efforts to overcome a series of difficulties, including the reduced water inflow to the basin, river navigation safety, power grid management, and hydropower unit maintenance, to the best of its ability. The Lancang River cascade hydropower stations have implemented emergency water scheduling and further increased the discharge flow from the Jinghong hydropower station to help alleviate the drought in Vietnam. At 8:00 a.m., on March 15, 2016, the discharge rate of the Jinghong hydropower station increased to 2,190 cubic meters per second, marking the official start of the emergency water discharge for the Lancang River cascade hydropower stations which have been implemented by China. Data shows that this emergency response has benefited five countries: Laos, Myanmar, Thailand, Cambodia, and Vietnam. Three days after the release, the water level of the Mekong River in the Chiang Saen area in northern Thailand rose from 2.3–2.5 meters to 3.29 meters.

Villagers in Vietnam expressed their heartfelt gratitude for China's assistance and said, "The small river in front of our doorstep finally has water again, and our small wooden boat is gradually floating. Our whole family sees hope." Mr. Syamphone, Minister of Natural Resources and Environment of Laos said, "A close neighbor is better than a distant relative. China is a responsible partner, and we will not forget China's help to the countries along the Mekong River."

Since 2019, the entire Lancang-Mekong River has been affected by climate change and has experienced continuous rainfall shortages, resulting in severe droughts in China and several other countries in the basin. The average amount of precipitation in the Lancang River in China was 728 millimeters, 34% less than normal, and the impoundment of relevant upstream reservoirs has reached the lowest level in recorded history. Yunnan has suffered the most severe droughts in the past decade due to factors such as the shortage of total precipitation, uneven spatial and temporal rainfall distribution, and less water inflow into the river's channels and reservoirs.

In spite of this, China has made every effort to ensure the reasonable downstream discharge of the Lancang River. At the request of Thailand and considering the serious drought in the Mekong River, China decided to increase the discharge flow rate of the Lancang River from 850 cubic meters per second to 1,000 cubic meters per second starting from January 24, 2020, in order to alleviate the urgent needs of Thailand and other countries located in the Mekong River Basin. Despite facing severe domestic drought conditions, China once again took special measures to overcome its own difficulties and increase the scale of its water discharge, making special arrangements within its capabilities to promote the overall interests of China and Thailand as close neighbors.

The road is not solitary and the whole world is one family. In response to droughts and disasters, China upholds the concept of a community with a shared future for humankind and timely extends a helping hand to its neighboring countries, which demonstrates China's proactive demeanor and responsibility as a global super power. Countries in the Mekong region generally believe that China's concepts and actions have become an important force to help disaster-stricken countries out of their darkest moments at urgent times, and establishing a community with a shared future for the countries in the Lancang-Mekong River is the right choice to address the common challenges of humankind and build a more prosperous and beautiful homeland.

Clear Up Doubts—the River of Mutual Trust Has a Powerful Source and Runs Long

There have been some false allegations against China made by foreign officials and non-governmental organizations regarding the governance of the upper and lower reaches of the Lancang-Mekong River. In 2020, a study funded by the US State Department claimed that China's damming and water storage facilities exacerbated the severe drought in Southeast Asia in 2019. The report, titled Monitoring the Quantity of Water Flowing through the Upper Mekong Basin Under Natural (Unimpeded) Conditions was published by an organization called Eye of the Earth.

However, data shows that the conclusion of the report was based on data from converting satellite measurement data from the Lancang River in Yunnan Province into a top soil moisture index, by which the report estimated the natural flow rate and concluded that the precipitation in Yunnan Province during the rainy season from May to October 2019 was slightly higher than the average level of previous years. However, in this research report, the author mainly used the model of moisture index developed by himself, which had been repeatedly mentioned by the author himself that such a model is not quite suitable for use in densely vegetated mountainous areas in his previous published papers. Nevertheless, the Lancang River is a mountainous area with very dense vegetation, so the applicability of the model that was used in the report is questionable.

Scholars from the Mekong River Commission have also stated that the drought in 2019 was largely due to significantly reduced precipitation during the rainy season, the delayed arrival and early departure of monsoon rains, abnormally high temperatures, and a higher evapotranspiration rate caused by the El Niño phenomenon, a preliminary analysis using the rainfall data and the observed date from 2008 to 2019 indicates. Therefore, it is groundless to blame China for the drought experienced by the downstream countries.

In addition, the inter-annual and seasonal variations in runoffs are very significant as the Mekong River is affected by Indian Ocean monsoons. After a drought in 2019, the water level of the Mekong River recovered in 2022. According to the monitoring data from the Mekong River Commission, compared with the "low flow" and drought in the same period during the past four years, the water volume of the Mekong River was the most abundant from January to April 2022 thanks to increased rainfall and discharges from upstream dams in China. These two factors have driven increased sediment and nutrient flows in the Mekong

River, which in turn have benefited fish supplies, agriculture development, and some 70 million people living along the river.

Meteorological indicators from the Mekong River Commission, from November 2021 to April 2022, show that the lower Mekong River Basin was not only wetter than in normal years (especially 2019 and 2020), but the accumulated precipitation in 2022 was about 25% higher than the average level across the entire basin. For example, in the upstream region, where China now provides data during the dry and rainy seasons, the Jinghong monitoring station shows that the water level in March and April was often higher than last year. At the Chiang Saen monitoring station in Thailand, the water level rose from 1.84 meters on March 2 to 3.25 meters on May 11. Although these numbers are lower than the average level in the years from 1961 to 2021, they are significantly higher than the average data of the dry years in the years from 2019 to 2021. The Vientiane monitoring station in Laos shows that the water level on March 2 and May 11 even exceeded the average level of the past 60 years and was significantly higher than the average level in 2019 and 2020. During the same period, the water level of monitoring stations from Stung Treng to Kampong Cham in Cambodia rose by 0.66–2.22 meters, which is about 1.5 meters higher than the same period last year. It can be concluded, and also shown from this data, that the rise in the water level of the Mekong River in 2022, and the rise and fall of the water level are mainly affected by the weather, especially precipitation, and the main cause of drought in the Lancang-Mekong River Basin, including Yunnan, is extreme weather, which is irrelevant to the construction of dams in China.

As is well known, hydroelectric power simply harnesses the power of water instead of consuming the total volume of water resources. However, these hydropower projects can also regulate natural runoffs. The hydraulic and hydropower projects developed and built by China on the Lancang River have always adhered to the principle of "reducing high flows and replenishing low flows." When a major flood occurs, a portion of the flood is then stored in reservoirs, which are then released in the dry season to replenish the flow.

On the one hand, this practice helps to alleviate flood pressure for people in downstream countries, and on the other hand, it meets the water needs of people living along the downstream river during dry seasons. The water yield of the Lancang River only accounts for about 15% of the total water resources in the Lancang-Mekong River, and China's current consumption of water resources only accounts for 1% of the total water resources in the entire basin, which not only indicates that the amount of water resources consumed by China in the upstream region has little impact on the downstream areas, but also suggests that China's responsibility and obligation to the downstream countries should not be exaggerated or even infinitely magnified.

The water from the Lancang-Mekong River stretches endlessly, nurturing the people of the six countries along its banks. Cooperation on water resources directly relates to the national economy and the livelihoods of the people in the six countries in the Lancang-Mekong region. Sharing one river like one family, we should uphold the principle of discussing and deciding together on important matters, strengthen upstream and downstream cooperation, take each other's concerns into consideration, continue to deepen practical cooperation in areas such as information sharing and people's livelihood projects and jointly improve the capability of intensive, efficient, and safe utilization of water resources in the Lancang-Mekong countries.

Tonle Sap Lake—the natural reservoir of the Mekong River

The Interconnectedness Promotes In-Depth Development and Cooperation

Since the launch of the LMC, the six countries along the river have always adhered to the original aspiration of "Shared River, Shared Future," joined hands to fight against the pandemic, promoted high-quality connectivity, vigorously carried out local cooperation, and jointly built livelihood projects. The LMC has maintained a high level of development and has successfully created a "golden sample" for regional cooperation. Thanks to the efforts of the six countries, high-standard, sustainable, and people-centered infrastructure connectivity projects have made significant progress, providing a strong impetus for economic development in the Lancang-Mekong Basin. Connectivity has become an important link in the development of the six countries. The China–Laos Railway, realized its dream of becoming a "land-linked" country, and serves as a precursor to future land interconnectivity projects among Lancang-Mekong countgries, such as the China–Thailand Railway. It is of great significance for the future connectedness of the entire Southeast Asian region and supports the high-quality construction of the Belt and Road Initiative and the implementation of the Global Development Initiative.

Railway Networks Draw the Indochina Peninsula Closer

With the sound of the "Song of China–Laos Friendship" and the command to "depart," on December 3, 2021, the China–Laos Railway was officially completed and put into operation on December 3, 2021. The "Fuxing" (Rejuvenation) and "Lancang–Mekong" trains ran in opposite directions, jointly constructing the emblem of the new era of China–Laos cooperation. After years of hard work and countless painstaking efforts, this ground-breaking project was finally completed. The opening and operation of the China–Laos Railway has ushered in a new era of railway transportation in Laos, profoundly changed the transportation landscape of the country, and fulfilled the long-cherished wish of Laos to transform from a "land-locked country" to a "land-linked country." As an important backbone of the Trans-Asian Railway, the China–Laos Railway will also become a "golden key" for Laos to connect with China in the north and Thailand, Malaysia, and other ASEAN countries in the south, which will have a positive impact on the China-ASEAN Free Trade Area and the LMC.

The China–Laos Railway—a Railway of Historic Significance

The China–Laos Railway is an electrified railway that connects Kunming Yunnan Province, China, with Vientiane, the capital city of Laos. It was constructed by China in accordance with the standard of Class I railroad and is the first cross-border railway mainly invested and constructed by China, jointly by the two countries and directly connected to the Chinese railway network.

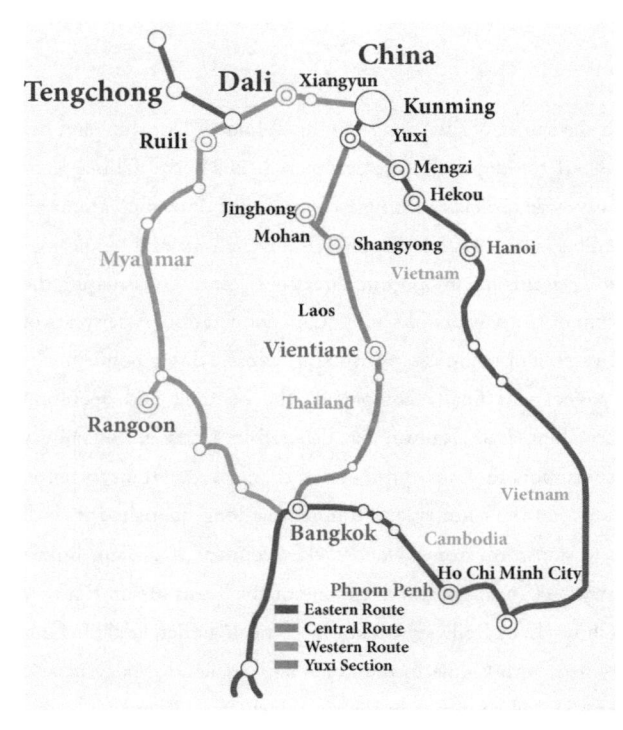

Map of the China–Laos Railway

A Train leaving the station

The railway is 1,035 kilometers long, starting from Kunming in the north, passing through Yuxi, Pu'er, and Xishuangbanna, before reaching Vientiane, the capital of Laos. It forms the main framework of the Trans-Asian Railway and is an important project that aligns China's Belt and Road Initiative with Laos' developmental strategy of transforming a "land-locked country" into a "land-linked country." It is also the first international railway primarily invested by China, fully utilizing Chinese technical standards and equipment, and directly connected to the Chinese railway network.

The China–Laos Railway consists of the Kunming–Yuxi section, the Yuxi–Mohan section, and the Boten–Vientiane section. Among them, the Kunming–Yuxi section is from Kunming South Railway Station to Yuxi Station, with a total length of 106 kilometers and a design speed of 200 km/h. The Yuxi–Mohan section runs from Yuxi Station to Mohan Station, with a total length of 507 kilometers and a design speed of 160 km/h. The Boten–Vientiane section runs from Moding Station to Vientiane South Station, with a total length of 422 kilometers and a design speed of 160 km/h. The China–Laos Railway has played an active role in facilitating convenient and efficient travel for the people of both countries, smoothing the dual circulation of dometic and international flows, and promoting the construction of the China–Laos Economic Corridor.

Hard Work Paves the Way to Success

Years of hard work have forged the quality of craftsmanship, aiming to bring blessings to the people of the region. On May 21, 2010, the construction of the Kunming–Yuxi section started, and the Boten–Vientiane section began on December 2, 2015. On April 19, 2016, the construction of the Yuxi–Mohan section started. On December 25 of the same year, a groundbreaking ceremony for the full-line construction of the China–Laos Railway was held. Finally, on December 3, 2021, the whole line was opened for operation.

There are many touching stories behind the success achieved so far. The Anding Tunnel is the longest tunnel in the whole line of the China–Laos Railway, which was co-constructed by China Railway No. 5 Engineering Group Co., Ltd. (CR5) and No. 19 Engineering Groups Co., Ltd. (CR19). With a total length of 17.5 kilometers, the tunnel had to penetrate a variety of complex geological structures. The difficulty and the scale of the project ranked among the forfront in the history of railway tunnel construction in China.

Li Fei, chief engineer of the Yuxi–Mohan Railway Project Department of the CR19, who was in charge of the tunnel exit construction at the exit end back then, recalled the dangerous situation at the end of 2018, "With a loud explosion, thousands of cubic meters of soil and rocks collapsed, and the tunnel was filled right behind three workers who were on a boring operation. They finally climbed out along a small gap through the ceiling of the hole."

At a point of 1.3-kilometer away from the exit end of the Anding Tunnel, the geological strata are mainly composed of carbonaceous mudstone and shale, which are very soft in texture and hard to shape when mixed with water; and the slurry formed posed a big challenge for the construction team. Sometimes they could only go ten meters some forward in one month. Meanwhile, the mud and water inrush in the tunnel were obstacles to completing the project on schedule. The engineers innovatively used large diameter pipe roof bolts and double-layered support control during the construction process to successfully overcome difficulties and ensure the project's progress. After years of hard work, the Anding Tunnel, the longest tunnel in the whole line of the China–Laos Railway, was finally completed in November 2020.

Based on the concept of ecological protection, the design engineers of the China–Laos Railway initially proposed more than 60 options covering three major directions, east, central, and west, trying to reduce the impact on the environment of the areas along the route. When selecting the railway route, the designers have taken into account the geological conditions, environmentally sensitive areas, etc. They have done comprehensive research on the track, long and short tunnels, river bridges, station locations, and other options to decide on an economical, reasonable, environmentally friendly, and overall feasible plan for the line.

The head of the overall design of the Chinese section from China Railway Eryuan Engineering Group stated that the engineers had consulted environmental protection and water conservancy departments along the routes, and the folks' voices were heard too. The route design has carefully referred to the results of the environmental impact assessment report and avoided core areas, buffer zones, and environmentally sensitive spots in various nature reserves, with the total length of the studied routes exceeding 14,000 kilometers.

For example, Yunnan has been the habitat of wild Asian elephants since ancient times. Since the railway passes through Xishuangbanna, the protection of wild Asian elephants aroused great public concern.

At the beginning of the route arrangement, the designers conducted detailed research on the living areas, distribution areas, and migration routes of wild elephants and analyzed the possible impact of the railroad construction on their habitat. The line was designed to avoid the living areas of wild elephants and to minimize the impact of the railroad construction and subsequent operation on their living environment by building longer tunnels, adjusting the location of the inclined shaft in the tunnel, and using rail bridges.

The Wild Elephant Valley Station on the China–Laos Railway is very close to the Asian Elephant Nature Reserve, and many relevant elements have been applied in the design of the station. For example, the top chandelier of the station, which is designed in the shape of a water-spouting elephant trunk and elephant footprints, has been well received by the public.

"Both ends of the station have been tunneled through, and the construction was finished underground, reducing the impact on the ecological environment, and after opening, the wild elephants' lives will not be affected as well," said Wang Junmin, project manager of the Wild Elephant Valley Station on the Yuxi–Mohan section, who is from the China Railway Construction Corporation. "The train runs quite smoothly on the China–Laos Railway, and it's very comfortable for passengers," said Wang Gengjie, chairman of the China Railway Group Kunming Bureau Group Co., Ltd.

Wild Asian elephants in Yunnan Province

Yexianggu (Wild Elephant Valley) Station—coming soon

Data Show the Popularity of China–Laos Railway

Since its opening on December 3, 2021, the China–Laos Railway has attracted much attention. By now, it has been obviously effective in promoting trade along the route, bringing great benefits to the people of both countries. The role of the "Golden Corridor" is increasingly visible. In the past two years since its opening, the China–Laos Railway has sent over 20 million passengers and more than 20 million tons of cargo.

The railroad has become a track of development, happiness, and friendship for Chinese and Laotian people. It not only brings great benefits to the people of the two countries but also provides a model for building the Belt and Road and promoting the construction of a community with a shared future for humankind. First, the railroad has made traveling convenient for people. The Fuxing and Lancang EMU trains have significantly shortened the traveling time between cities along the route, which are favored by the people of both countries as their first choice for travel. The monthly passenger traffic on the entire China–Laos Railway has increased from around 600,000 in the early stage of opening to more than 1.1 million in December 2023, according to Xinhua News Agency. In the Chinese section, 51 passenger trains were sent daily on average, with the single-day traffic peaking at the highest at 83,000 and a total of 20.46 million passengers traveled by rail. In the Lao section, now there are 10 passenger trains running, up from 4 trains a day at the beginning, and the highest number of passengers sent daily reaches 10,197, and the total number of passengers amounts to 3.74 million. The railway has brought great convenience to the Laotian people. Second, cargo transportation is highly efficient. Its operation data has reached new record highs. As of December 27, 2023, the China–Laos Railway transport continues to run stably in security, with a cumulative total of 30.33 million tons of goods transported, among which the cross-border cargo exceeded 6.2 million tons, and more than 2,700 types of cargo were transported.

At the same time, there are innovative lines, such as "Lancang-Mekong Express," the "China–Laos Railway + China–Europe Railway," "Shanghai–Kunming

Lancang-Mekong Express," and the China–Laos International Cold-Chain Train. There are 14 cross-border cargo trains running every day as of December 2023, a big increase from the 2 trains daily at the initial stage of operation. Third, the subsequent effects are obvious. In the past year since the opening of China–Laos Railway, it has promoted regional interconnectedness and created a win-win situation for the two countries, bringing authentic opportunities and benefits to enterprises and people in China, Laos, and nearby ASEAN countries, and promoting the expansion and development of various industries along the railroad. The output of iron ore, cassava flour, rubber, etc., in Laos has increased significantly. The business ties and trades in the region have been advanced as well. Cross-border cargo delivered by the China–Laos Railway has gone to Laos, Thailand, Myanmar, Malaysia, Cambodia, Vietnam, Bangladesh, Singapore, and other countries that are co-building the Belt and Road, and the cargo categories have been expanded from around 10 kinds of goods like fertilizers and general merchandise at the initial stage of operation to more than 2,700 categories such as electronics, photovoltaic products, and cold-chain fruit by the end of 2023.

Freight data (100 days)

2 trains	6 trains	over 120 MT
Average daily cross-border cargo trains	Cross-border cargo trains in peak operation	Total amount of goods transported
18 mn	360 trains	
Passengers sent	Cumulative number of cross-border cargo trains	

Data of the China–Laos Railway in its first 100 days of operation

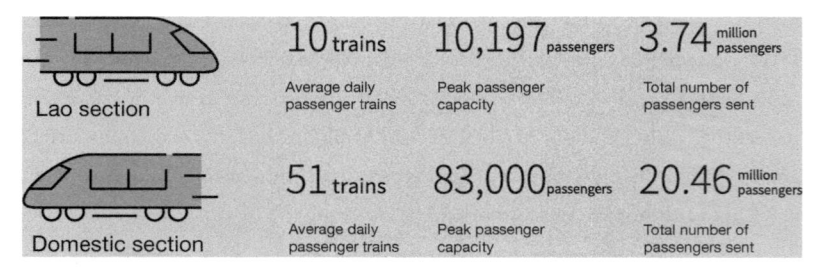

Lao section

10 trains	10,197 passengers	3.74 million passengers
Average daily passenger trains	Peak passenger capacity	Total number of passengers sent

Domestic section

51 trains	83,000 passengers	20.46 million passengers
Average daily passenger trains	Peak passenger capacity	Total number of passengers sent

Operations of the China–Laos Railway at a glance (2 years)

International Freight Trains Promote Regional Development

On December 21, 2021, the first China–Laos international freight train from Vientiane South Station in Laos to Tengjun International Land Port in Kunming, Yunnan province of China was the prelude to innovative development.

On June 8, 2022, a special train for Qingling Motors carrying 40 light trucks slowly departed from Chongqing Tuanjiecun Railway Station. Chongqing and Kunming Customs facilitated the international freight train to leave China through the Mohan Railway Port using combined rail transport to move the cargo to Vientiane South Station in Laos. The smooth operation of this international freight train has boosted the exports of made-in-Chongqing products and further accessed the Southeast Asian market.

In addition to industrial products such as automobiles, the opening of the China–Laos Railway has further facilitated the imports and exports of agricultural products at home and abroad.

Located on the west bank of the Mekong River, Sayaboury Province in Laos abounds with double cropping rice, peanuts, cassava, and so on. Cassava, one of the world's major tubers, is widely grown in tropical and subtropical regions.

In the tropical as well as subtropical regions of southwestern China, cassava is among the top five crops in the area, after rice, sweet potato, sugarcane, and corn, and plays a very important role in industrial applications and feed production.

On the morning of June 11, 2022, a freight train loaded with 30 TEUs of high-quality cassava flour weighing 395 tons setting off from Vientiane arrived at Huaihua, Hunan Province, waiting for unloading. This train marks the first time that the Huaihua international dry port of Hunan Province has the transportation

The China–Laos Railway stretching across forests and lands

and distribution capacity for ASEAN bulk commodities, laying a solid foundation for Hunan Province and the central and western regions to import mahogany boards, rubbers, and other bulk resource products from Southeast Asia. This is a milestone for further building an unimpeded economic corridor that connects RCEP regions and promotes the development of Huaihua's export-oriented economy, which plays a significant role in drawing China's internal regions and provinces to participate in the LMC.

As of October 2023, a total of 25 provinces (autonomous regions and municipalities) across the country have launched the China–Laos freight trains and carried cargo to more than ten countries and regions such as Laos, Thailand, Myanmar, Vietnam, Malaysia, etc. The China–Laos railway has woven a big trade network stretching to Southeast Asia. The freight trains back-and-forth have built a bridge connecting China with the Southeast Asian region.

The railroad will lead to a long-lasting friendship between China and Laos, and the LMC will continue to develop in-depth because of this railroad, which will release greater vitality in the future.

Oil and Gas to Home—Energy Cooperation

By June 8, 2020, China and Myanmar have established diplomatic relations for 70 years. On June 3, 2010, as an important achievement of the 60th anniversary of the establishment of diplomatic relations between China and Myanmar, the construction of the China-Myanmar oil and gas pipeline officially started. After ten years of hard work, a world-class, high-quality pipeline project and an international channel of oil and gas transit were completed on schedule, which plays a significant role in adjusting the economic structure in Southwest China and diversifying energy import of China. At the same time, it has accelerated the economic development and the oil and gas industry progress along the Myanmar pipeline, improving local people's livelihood. The China-Myanmar oil and gas pipeline has become a pilot demonstration of the implementation of the Belt and Road Initiative in Myanmar and an authentic witness of the China-Myanmar Pauk-Phaw (fraternal) friendship in the new era.

China-Myanmar Oil and Gas Pipeline

The China-Myanmar oil and gas pipeline is China's fourth largest energy import passage following the Central Asia gas pipeline, the China-Russia crude oil pipeline and maritime shipping routes. It includes crude oil pipelines and natural gas pipelines, which can transport crude oil from the southwest to China without passing through Malacca Strait. The China-Myanmar crude oil pipeline starts from Madè Island, a small island southeast of Kyaukpyu Port on the west coast of Myanmar, where the natural gas pipeline starts.

The launch of the China-Myanmar Crude Oil Pipeline Project has shaped up the strategic layout of four crude oil and gas import channels for China: the China-Russia crude oil pipeline in the northeast, the Central Asia natural gas pipeline in the northwest, the China-Myanmar oil and gas pipeline in the southwest, and maritime shipping routes through the Malacca Strait, which is conducive to diversify oil transportation channels and ensure the security of China's energy supply. The pipeline is helpful for easing China's dependence on the Malacca Strait and reducing the risk of importing crude oil by sea.

At present, the majority of China's imported crude oil enters the country by shipping routes through the Strait of Malacca. The China-Myanmar crude oil pipeline has opened up an important land passage in the southwest for oil and gas imports. This newly added route of crude oil imports is helpful for enhancing the oil supply security in China.

Domestically in China, the crude oil pipeline is 1,631 kilometers long and the natural gas pipeline totaled at 1,727 kilometers, with 771 kilometers located in Myanmar. There will be 12 billion cubic meters of natural gas transited through the gas pipelines and 22 million tons of crude oil through the oil pipeline annually. Myanmar's section is 771 kilometers.

Four Countries and Six Companies—Scientific Management to Dispel Worries

The China-Myanmar Oil and Gas Pipeline Project is an international cooperation participated by six companies from China, Myanmar, South Korea, and India. The entire project covers China-Myanmar crude oil and natural gas pipelines and supporting crude oil terminals. Since the project is being constructed in Myanmar, and different countries and companies are involved, effective management and coordination among all parties are vital to ensure the steady progress of the project. During the construction process, the Southeast Asia Pipeline Company of CNPC (China National Petroleum Corporation) has followed the corresponding international rules and practices, adopted a reasonable management model, and made the project a model for international cooperation projects.

Faced with doubts and smears, China has always adhered to information transparency and accepted supervision from all investing countries. Three press conferences were held in Myanmar to positively respond to various issues like pipeline safety, environmental protection, and compensation for land occupation, which were concerned by the people in the construction area. Besides, the China-Myanmar Oil and Gas Pipeline Project Manual is revised annually in Chinese, English, and Burmese to ensure that investors can track the progress of the construction. As for the land occupation in the areas along the pipeline, China's relevant parties have always adhered to the standardized approach by negotiating with the local government, relevant investors and partners, and the people whose land was occupied, reasonable compensation plans were formulated to ensure that the interests of the owner of the occupied land will not be harmed. The China-Myanmar Oil and Gas Pipeline Project has been in construction and operation in Myanmar for more than a decade and has been fully recognized by all parties.

The China-Myanmar oil and gas pipeline

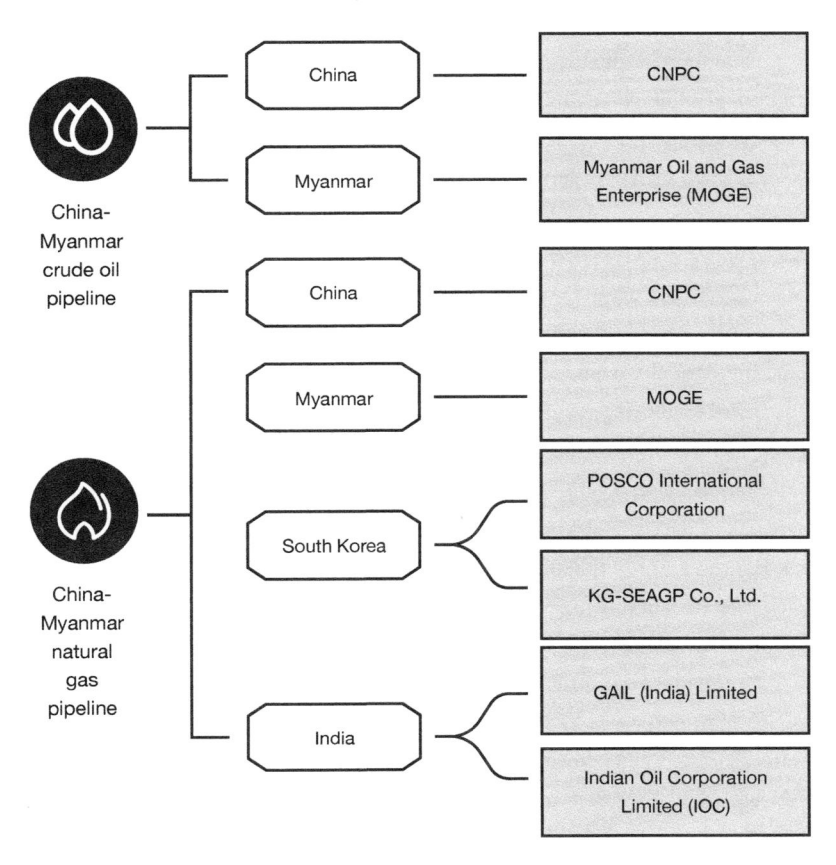

Investors of China-Myanmar Oil & Gas Pipeline Project

China-Myanmar Cooperation for a Brilliant Win-Win Future

The pipelines for natural gas and crude oil are laid in parallel and the whole line traverses the four provinces and states of Myanmar and finally enters China through Ruili City in Yunnan Province. As soon as the oil and gas pipelines are completed and put into use, they will not only ensure the stability of the regional energy supply but also stimulate the construction of the oil and gas industry and infrastructure and boost the economic strength of the southwest region of China, Yunnan Province included.

As an important energy infrastructure in Myanmar, the China-Myanmar oil and gas pipeline plays a huge role in promoting Myanmar's economic and social development. Myanmar has a superior geographical location and rich natural resources since ancient times. However, affected by geopolitics, history, religion, and technology, its economic development has been relatively slow in recent decades. Faced with the severe shortage of power supply and gas, the country is in dire need of energy infrastructure.

Forty days after the official commissioning of the China-Myanmar gas pipeline, the natural gas power plant at the Kyaukpyu station successfully supplied and distributed gas-generated power to the people in Kyaukpyu region, who have since said goodbye to the dark days and lived a bright life. At the same time, as Myanmar is also one of the investors of the project, based on the previous agreement, once the pipeline is officially put into operation, two million tons of crude oil and 20% of the total volume of natural gas will be supplied for Myanmar each year, thus improving the economic development and living standards of the people in the region.

As the first large-scale energy project in the Mekong region and the largest energy industry project in Southeast Asia, the successful completion and commissioning of the China-Myanmar oil and gas pipeline has promoted China-ASEAN energy cooperation and initially realized energy pipeline interconnection, further facilitated regional economic development, enhancing complementary advantages, and setting an example for the subsequent development of the Bangladesh-China-India-Myanmar Economic Corridor.

Chen Hai, Chinese Ambassador to Myanmar, said, "The China-Myanmar Oil and Gas Pipeline Project is an important achievement of China-Myanmar cooperation under the Belt and Road Initiative background and has played an important role in the development of Myanmar and cooperation between the two nations."

On July 28, 2013, the China-Myanmar gas pipeline started operation and transmitted natural gas to the Burmese market through its distribution stations. As of May 25, 2020, the China-Myanmar Oil and Gas Pipeline Project has delivered a total of 30 million tons of crude oil and approximately 26.5 billion cubic meters of natural gas to China, and 4.6 billion cubic meters of natural gas to Myanmar. As of May 2020, the China-Myanmar oil and gas pipeline has brought Myanmar a cumulative direct economic revenue of about US$514 million, including US$252 million for the natural gas pipeline project and US$262 million for the crude oil pipeline project. In addition, by July 2022, the Dehong Oil and Gas Transmission Branch of Southwest Oil and Gas Pipeline Co., Ltd., the first operating company of the China-Myanmar Oil and Gas Pipeline, has safely transported more than 35 billion standard cubic meters of natural gas and more than 50 million tons of crude oil.

"The China-Myanmar oil and gas pipeline has solved successfully opened up the downstream markets for Myanmar's natural gas, not only creating more jobs and generating foreign exchanges, but also bringing considerable economic benefits including tax revenue and investment dividends," said U Win Kai, Myanmar's Minister of Electricity and Energy.

Heroes behind the Success

Madè Island, an untouched island near Kyaukpyu, lying quietly on the sea, covers about 12 square kilometers. No one could have imagined that this obscure island lying quietly above sea level would one day become the starting point of a great energy cooperation project. According to Zhang Jicheng, deputy director of the Management Office of Madè Island in Kyaukpyu, the entire island was almost barren before the construction of the China-Myanmar Oil and Gas Pipeline Project.

Zhang Jicheng, born in 1981 and graduated from Xi'an University of Petroleum and joined the China Petroleum Pipeline Engineering Co., Ltd., in 2023 is one of the earliest participants in the construction of the China-Myanmar Oil and Gas Pipeline Project. In 2009, Zhang became a member of the preparatory team for Project. In the following decade, he participated in the entire construction process and witnessed the project from start to finish.

Zhang Jicheng first came to Madè Island for the project survey in 2009 and recalled, "The island was surrounded by sea, and as far as the eye could see, it was barren and basically in a pristine state. The base site is located in the southeast of the island, and several villages are scattered in the northwest. Except for a few small pieces of cultivated land that have been reclaimed by the villagers, the rest of the island was overgrown with shrubs and full of insects."

On June 3, 2010, the construction of the China-Myanmar oil and gas pipeline officially began in the presence of Wen Jiabao and Thein Sein. Technically speaking, the builders actually started their pioneering journey to Madè Island in 2009. They had to travel by various means of transportation to get to the final destination: first flying to Yangon, then transferring to Kyaukpyu, and then taking a boat from Kyaukpyu to Madè Island. Due to the poor infrastructure, there was no pier on the island, and they had to walk in seawater to get to the shore, and their building work started alongside the mudflats. The island was short of power supply, fresh water, and Internet, and the climate there was also harsh, yet the builders stood fast on this isolated island over 2,000 kilometers away from their motherland, supported by the spirit of hard work, fearlessness, dedication, and truthseaking.

Liu Dong, the head of Madè Island station, recalled that when he first came to the island, he thought there were normal accommodation buildings. But what he saw were rows of board houses with blue roofs and white walls. "I have my own pillows, but the beds and sheets belong to someone else's. My highest record was moving nine times a month, and my luggage was never opened. The rooms were not soundproof, so I could raise my voice to talk to the person next door. The summer was extremely hot, and in the rainy season, bean-sized raindrops fell on the tin roof, and the noise was like someone was demolishing a house." In 2014, the office and accommodation areas were completed and they finally got their own dormitory. With the construction process, Madè evolved from a temporary camp to an island with permanent office buildings and a dock, which brought vitality and warmth to the hardships of construction work.

Although the environment on the island was harsh, the builders did not give in but rather "rolled up their sleeves to do more," which demonstrates responsibility, a commitment to a mission, and patriotism in their young hearts! The completion of the project not only enhances the energy cooperation between China and Myanmar but also changes the living environment of the people in Kyaukpyu to a great extent and completes the first major energy cooperation project under the LMC mechanism, which provides a reference for future international cooperation in the energy area under the Mekong cooperation mechanism.

Energy cooperation between China and Myanmar in the energy sector has been developing, and the sharing of oil and gas resources has not only ensured China's energy security, but also brought economic benefits to the people of Myanmar. The LMC is broadening its horizons because of this pipeline and will play a more valuable role in the future.

A panoramic view of Madè Island

Power Supplies Support Regional Cooperation

With a total length of 4,880 kilometers and a total basin area of 810,000 square kilometers, the Lancang-Mekong River is known as the "Danube of the East." Its mainstream has a total drop of 5,167 meters, and its basin area is rich in shipping, irrigation, hydropower, and other resources, forming a treasure house in Yunnan, China, and Southeast Asia. The theoretical reserves of hydropower resources are 36.56 million kilowatts, with a development potential of 23.48 million kilowatts, of which 20.88 million kilowatts come from the mainstream, accounting for 89% of the entire basin.

A favorable regional cooperation environment lays the foundation for deepening cooperation in cross-border power generation and supply. The Mekong countries share the principles of "good neighborliness, development first, creating mutual benefit and win-win results, and putting the people's well-being first." The governments and enterprises involved have established a good foundation and are in urgent need of cooperation, and China has devised a model for cooperation with the Mekong countries in trade, water resources cooperation, the fight against pandemics, and the people's welfare. In November 2021, China and ASEAN established a comprehensive strategic partnership. Under the framework of the LMC mechanism, the Mekong countries will have broader prospects for cooper-

The groundbreaking ceremony of Para Substation

ation in social progress, economic development, and trade. The development and cooperation of all parties in a more transparent manner will also require energy and power support.

Para Substation of Laos

In September 2021, when the weather was still hot in Vientiane, the capital of Laos, the Para substation (500 kV) was under construction by a Chinese team, and it was almost finished. The project was undertaken by a Chinese power company.

The 500 kV power transmission project in Laos (Chuang Khouang–Nasai Thong section) is an important project planned by the Laotian government under the Seventh Five-Year Plan. Under the Belt and Road Initiative and with the deepening of the LMC mechanism, the connectivity cooperation between China and the Mekong countries has further developed, with energy connectivity being one of the important sectors. The aim of the Para Substation Project is to promote power interconnectedness between China and Laos, and it's the first 500 kV electrical transmission and transformation project in Laos.

As an important site of the project, the 500 kV Para Substation is an important part of the 500 kV high-voltage transmission line network project that has been planned for ten provinces in north central Laos. With three main transformers and a total capacity of 750 MVA, when completed and put into use, it will help Laos establish a cross-border power transmission corridor with a large-capacity and high-efficiency, embarking on the strategic goal of creating an Accumulator in Southeast Asia and serving to open an efficient power transmission corridor through China, Laos, Thailand, and Vietnam.

"The Para substation project started in 2017, and it will open an efficient power transmission corridor through China, Laos, Thailand, and Vietnam after completion," said Xu Mingliang, the Chinese head of the construction company for the Para project. Xu was working with the Guangxi Power Transmission and Transformation Power Southern.

In recent years, similar transnational energy cooperation projects have been launched in the Mekong countries, such as the BOT projects of the No. 1 Namtha River Hydropower Plant in Laos and the Phase One Vinh Tan Coal Power Plant in Vietnam, which are all high-quality power projects participated in by Chinese power enterprises.

"Such kind of cooperation has advanced the green development of regional energy. In recent years we have also held several power technology training and seminars according to the needs of power enterprises in neighboring countries to further promote and deepen cooperation in related areas," said Wu Baoying, chairman of the Energy Development Institute of China Power Southern Grid.

After the official signing of the Regional Comprehensive Economic Partnership Agreement, the demand for energy cooperation between China and ASEAN countries has further increased, and the prospects are bright. The foundation for cooperation between China and the Mekong countries is sound, and a good platform for energy cooperation is provided by the LMC mechanism. At the 18th China-ASEAN Expo, participants from all walks of life believed that there was a good foundation for cooperation in power and other energy industries for China and ASEAN countries, and further deepening energy cooperation would help promote regional economic growth and improve social welfare. Electrical power cooperation between China and Laos can be seen as a demonstration project and provides a reference for future energy ventures between China and the Mekong countries.

The China–Laos Railway External Power Supply Project

Connecting the two countries, the China–Laos Railway runs directly from Kunming in the north to Vientiane, the capital of Laos, in the south. The Laotian section of the track has a total length of 422 kilometers and shapes the backbone of the Pan–Asia Railway. As the first railway in a practical sense in Laos, it is also a landmark achievement for China's overseas cooperation under the LMC, which corresponds to the objectives of the Belt and Road Initiative. It is also the first overseas railway financed by China as the major investor, designed and built according to Chinese standards, built with Chinese equipment, and connected to China's domestic railway network. To ensure the orderly operation of the railway, it is very important to ensure a stable power supply, including the Laotian section as well. The power supply project of the Laotian section has been built using Chinese technical standards and equipment for the whole line, so it can guarantee the power supply for the operation of the high-speed electrified railway.

The overall length of the China–Laos Railway external power supply project spanned for 936.8 kilometers, divided into Chinese and Laotian sections, which were invested, constructed, operated, and maintained by the China Southern Power Grid Corporation and the Laos-China Power Investment Company, respectively. Three new 220 kV switch yard and thirty-five 220 kV lines have been built into the Chinese section to provide reliable electricity for fourteen traction substations. In the Laotian section, twenty new 115 kV lines and eleven 115 kV substation intervals have been built. Ten traction substations for the electrified railway have been connected to the Laotian national grid.

More than half of the Laotian section is located in mountainous areas. In order to protect the ecological environment along the line, the construction workers have applied a variety of technologies. For example, when erecting steel pylons, differentiated leg length technology, also known as unequal height foundations, has been used to determine the length of the four tower legs based on the height difference of the original terrain on which the legs stand, which means only four footholds for the tower need to be cleared for construction, minimizing the damage to the vegetation. Upon completion, local grass seeds were sown to restore the original ecology.

The whole project lasted for twelve months, and the highest temperature reached 40°C. Six hundred fifty-four builders from China and Laos worked hard under the scorching sun and pouring rains and finally finished the project successfully. As a supporting project serving the construction of a China–Laos Community with a Shared Future, the successful completion of the power supply project has guaranteed the orderly operation of the China–Laos Railway. However, the sudden outbreak of the COVID-19 pandemic in 2020 has brought great challenges to the project.

One participant of the project recalled, "Tight schedules and heavy workloads, plus the onset of the sudden pandemic. Our plan was completely disrupted, and I was really worried that we wouldn't be able to finish." Yet neither the pandemic prevention and control, nor the project construction should be taken lightly. Six hundred and fifty-four staff from both China and Laos raced against time to constantly advance the project.

Due to COVID-19, the project had to be postponed for three months to ensure the health of the staff. Yet the very three months were the dry season for Laos, the golden season of construction. When the project resumed, the rainy season came, and it rained almost every day. The land on the construction site was flooded, and some potholes turned into ponds. Most often, the construction work could only get back on track after the ponds were drained.

"It's no exaggeration. The pounding was as deep as fishponds." Yang Lumin, head of the fourth construction unit of the Laotian section in the China–Laos Railway external power supply project, recalled the situation at that time.

The northern part of Laos is mountainous and has a lack of infrastructure. Continuous heavy rain made the roads rather slippery, and cars couldn't pass at all. All the materials could only be transported manually.

On March 18, 2020, four construction teams witnessed their first concrete pouring for the foundation of the steel pylons, which meant a full resumption of work. However, due to the continuous spread of the pandemic in Laos, on March 29, Laos shut down the whole country, and a "ground order" was implemented. The project was forced into suspension. It was not until May 4 that the construction staff got back to their jobs after the pandemic was brought under control to a certain extent.

Wang Fude, senior business manager of the Laos-China Power Investment Company, has experienced the whole process of construction, suspension, and resumption. "It's like riding a roller coaster. We worked quickly in the period of time before the flooding season, coordinated the required preliminary work village by village, and completed the preparation procedures for 356 steel pylons so that the project could be carried out on schedule in an orderly manner and completed smoothly."

Huang Wengang, general manager of the Laos-China Power Investment Company and director of the external power supply project of the Laotian section, was excited, "We have finally caught up." The word "catch" up is oversimplified, and behind it lie the efforts and friendships of 654 Chinese and Laotian employees. The word embodied the "hard work" of the project teams from both countries. With their joint efforts, the China–Laos construction personnel not only made up for the delay caused by the pandemic, but also ensured "zero security incidents and zero infections," with none of the 654 workers infected with the coronavirus.

As an important interconnection project under the LMC, the China–Laos Railway has not only brought the two countries closer, but also built emotional connections among the project staff. More than 80% of the employees were Laotian people. Because of the language barrier, the team could barely communicate in the beginning. But by the end, the employees from both sides cheered together for the completion of the project and forged deep friendships.

Through cooperation in power, China and the Mekong countries have built a bridge of interconnection and ensured smooth regional cooperation and energy security. The project also benefited people in the Lancang-Mekong region. Thousands of families and homes were lit up.

Engineering personnel of the Yunnan Power Transmission and Transformation Company conducting an inspection on a steel pylons

Connected Land and Sea Navigate to a New Direction

Now that all countries are paying close attention to the post-pandemic economic recovery, the New International Land-Sea Trade Corridor has emerged and kept developing to ensure a smooth and stable supply chain and the foreign trade of the Mekong countries. This important corridor connecting ASEAN and Eurasia covers all provinces, autonomous regions and cities in western China and will bring great benefits to the Lancang-Mekong region. Under the LMC mechanism, it will further promote interconnection and cooperation among the Mekong countries by broadening regional connectivity and development. It will provide a new drive for the post-pandemic economic recovery in the region, pointing to a new direction of future interconnection and development for the LMC.

The first freight train of the China–Laos Railway (Chengdu–Chongqing–Vientiane) through the New Land-Sea Trade Corridor

The Land-Sea Corridor Strengthens Regional Connectivity

The New Western Land-Sea Corridor passes through the entire western region of China and connects the five countries along the Mekong River and other Southeast Asian countries with China through multimodal transport (rail/sea/road). At the same time, it leads into Central Asia and Europe in the north. The Silk Road Economic Belt is connected to the 21st Century Maritime Silk Road. It is a comprehensive international trade channel integrating regional manufacturing chains and supply chains, land and sea cargo collection, and customs clearance efficiency. Faced with the new trend of regional integration, the corridor will quickly integrate with the LMC by exporting products from the Mekong countries to the Central Asian and European markets via central and western Chinese markets, which will greatly logistic time needed for transportation. The New Land-Sea Corridor, officially kicked off in September 2017 and was initially co-constructed by Chongqing, Guangxi, Guizhou, and Gansu in western China. In August 2019, China released an overall plan about the country's New Western Land-Sea Corridor, which recognized the corridor as part of its national strategy.

The Mekong countries have actively strengthened their connectivity in recent years, which has laid a solid foundation for the interconnection of the Western Land-Sea Corridor and the LMC mechanism. In railway construction, the China–Laos Railway has been operating successfully, and the channel for inter-modal transportation via this railway is on the right track. Besides, the Chinese section of the China–Vietnam Railway has adopted standard gauges and is fully electrified. What's more, the China–Myanmar Railway is proceeding well, and the preliminary work for the China–Myanmar–India Railway has begun. In terms of road transportation, more than 20 international passenger and freight routes from China to Laos, Vietnam, Thailand, etc., are in operation, which has gradually formed an extensive network with major border cities as nodes in the center and border ports as junctions, and this is very beneficial for the surrounding countries. In terms of water transport, normal navigation has been achieved among the four countries of China, Thailand, Laos, and Myanmar. The multi-modal transportation network has laid the foundation for the connection between the Mekong countries and the Western Land-Sea Corridor, which thereby further facilitates the inter-connectivity of different countries under the LMC mechanism.

Before the official kickoff of the Western Land-Sea Corridor, cargo from the Mekong countries could only be transported by sea to the eastern coast of China and then transferred to the west via the Yangtze River or by road, or by road-rail or sea-road-rail inter-modal transport. The process usually takes more than a month. The opening of the New Land-Sea Corridor has saved more than ten days in logistic time.

An Unimpeded New Corridor

Since the opening and operation of the New Western Land-Sea Corridor, it has been operating from one to two trains per month to a weekly train on a regular basis, and then to one train daily and even more than ten trains per day. In 2023, trains through the New Western Land-Sea Corridor transported a total of 861,000 TEUs of cargo, a year-on-year growth rate of 13.8%. Up to now, the new corridor has reached 120 countries and regions and 486 ports around the world, transporting over 900 categories of commodities.

The Western Land-Sea Corridor has kept expanding from traditional logistics services to a comprehensive system covering trade, manufacturing, finance, and data, and the service quality has been continuously improved. With this logistics corridor, special agricultural and sideline products such as citrus from the Three Gorges, traditional Chinese medicine from the Northwest, and vegetables from inland cities can reach overseas markets more conveniently, and they have become the best endorsement of Chinese quality. Along this corridor, more products from the Mekong countries have also entered the Chinese market, meeting the various needs of Chinese consumers. For example, Basa fish from Vietnam, durian from Thailand, and cassava flour from Laos have been welcomed at more dinner tables because of their freshness and competitive prices.

On the world map, the New Land-Sea Corridor connects the Indochina Peninsula in the south and runs through western China, and then it links to the transcontinental China Railway Express in Eurasia.

The electronic products made in LG Group's Vietnamese factory arrive in Chongqing via the New Land-Sea Corridor and then get transferred to the China Railway Express heading for Europe. German goods are delivered to the Southeast Asian market by the China-Europe freight train and the New Land and Sea Corridor. Both trips take less than half of the shipping time using ocean transport.

Since 2021, good news keeps coming from the New Western Land and Sea Corridor. The first international Chengdu-Chongqing-Vientiane freight train departed on December 4, 2021. By now, the China–Laos Railway has been operating on a regular basis.

This new corridor strengthens the links between China and the Mekong countries as well as other regions, which will help further promote the LMC and provide a strong guarantee for regional economic development.

People loading Hami melons in Xinjiang

Refrigerated trucks heading for Bangkok via the New Land-Sea Corridor (Xinjiang–Chongqing–Thailand)

A Quick Customs Clearance Model Facilitates the LMC

On May 21, 2021, an international freight train full of foodstuffs and agricultural machinery whistled loudly and departed from Chongqing. It would arrive in Vientiane, the capital of Laos, four days later. This train was the first to take advantage of the brand-new quick customs clearance model which is used for the New International Land-Sea Trade Corridor in China.

The quick customs clearance system is a new model mainly designed for rail freight containers by the General Administration of Customs. This further simplifies customs clearance procedures, improves transportation efficiency, and ensures the smooth flow of international cargo. This model will reduce clearance time by one to two days, and the single container transport costs will also be cut by more than RMB 200. On May 20, 2021, for the first time, the cross-border train from Vientiane finished its customs clearance using this quick model, entered China through the Mohan Port, and arrived in Chongqing smoothly one day earlier than before ushering in a new era of quick customs clearances and two-way trips of China–Laos international freight trains through the New International Land-Sea Trade Corridor.

As of September 2023, Chongqing has operated a total of 420 China–Laos freight trains, transporting 9,600 TEUs with a total value of RMB 1.415 billion.

The quick customs clearance model will essentially ease the pressure on customs clearance at ports, further smooth the international logistics passage, and accelerate the efficient operation of international trains in the New International Land-Sea Trade Corridor. The application of quick customs clearance is conducive to the interconnection of countries under the LMC mechanism. The model will further lower the cost of customs clearance and improve transportation efficiency. The problem of prolonged traveling time on the Kunming–Vientiane road due to the slow process of customs clearance will be resolved effectively. Based on that, the transportation of cargo among the Mekong countries will be more convenient, and China will have better interconnectedness with the region.

The New Western Land-Sea Corridor, a groundbreaking new route, will be more powerful in the future. It will further promote the smooth integration of LMC and the construction of the New International Land-Sea Trade Corridor, consistently unleashing new opportunities and facilitating the in-depth advancement of LMC and regional connectivity.

The first returned train of the China–Laos Railway (Vientiane–Chongqing) departing from China

The first China–Laos Railway train following the quick customs clearance and leaving China

LMC Empowered by the Energy Cooperation and the Upgrading of Production Capacity

S ince the LMC's inception, remarkable results have been achieved, and collaboration among the Mekong countries has made them more resilient to risks and brought about promising economic growth.

The surging water of the Lancang-Mekong River has long been nourishing the drainage basins. It has brought a huge number of resources and enormous amounts of energy to people living there. With resources that are aligned toward production capacities, and the existence of these opportunities that lead to development, the countries along the river are expecting a better tomorrow.

Energies Lay the Foundation for Cooperation

In general, production capacity refers to the number of products or the number of raw materials that one enterprise can manufacture or handle within a planned period under established organizational and technical conditions, with all the fixed assets involved in production. It represents both the productivity and the scale of an enterprise, and also how sustainable it is. Production capacity has been one of the focuses since the initiation of the LMC.

The Lancang-Mekong upgrading of production capacity is part of the cooperation in international production capacity. It focuses on building, transferring and upgrading of production capacity to support mutually beneficial international industrial investment. Being market-oriented, the enterprises, as the major participants, mainly have direct investment, contract engineering, the trading of equipment, and technical cooperation to develop the manufacturing industry, infrastructure, resource, and energy sectors.

According to the Joint Statement on Production Capacity Cooperation among Lancang-Mekong Countries, production capacity cooperation is carried out from five aspects as follows:

- First, formulate an Action Plan for Production Capacity Cooperation among Lancang-Mekong Countries.
- Second, enhancing the capacity-building for productivity improvement and conducting experience exchange and training.

- Third, explore the possibility to set up platforms for production capacity and investment cooperation, hold activities including the Production Capacity Cooperation Forum for Lancang-Mekong countries, and try to establish an alliance for promoting production capacity and investment cooperation among the Lancang-Mekong countries.
- Fourth, encourage enterprises and financial institutions from the Lancang-Mekong countries to participate in production capacity cooperation.
- Fifth, to set up a multi-lateral Development Fund for LMC Production Capacity Cooperation.

The scale and quality of cooperation in regional production capacity have been rising since the launch of the LMC. There has been a big increase in intra-regional trade and investment. According to the United Nations Department of Economic and Social Affairs statistics, the trade relations between China and the five Mekong countries have changed and shown some trends. On the one hand, there is a closer trading connection between China and the five Mekong countries. China has become the largest importer of Cambodia, Myanmar, and Vietnam and the largest exporter of Laos and Myanmar. On the other hand, trade relations among Cambodia, Laos, Thailand, Myanmar, and Vietnam have developed significantly, with Thailand becoming the largest importer of Laos, the second largest importer of Cambodia, and Vietnam being the third largest exporter of Cambodia, Laos, etc. The increasingly close trade relations among the Mekong countries have laid a solid foundation for production capacity and investment cooperation between China and the five Mekong countries. China's trade with the five Mekong countries reached US$416.7 billion in 2022, 5% up year-on-year.

Since the launch of LMC, the total economic output of the five Mekong countries has been steadily increasing, with a year-on-year growth rate of more than 40%, and the level of economic and social development has been continuously rising. China is the largest trading partner for Vietnam, Cambodia, Myanmar, and Thailand, the second largest trading partner for Laos, and in return, Vietnam has become China's fourth largest trading partner. At the same time, China has provided special loans for production cooperation, and it has supported more than 40 major infrastructure projects in the Mekong countries, including the new international airport in Siem Reap (Cambodia), the power grid renovation in Vientiane (Laos), and the coal-fired power plant in Vinh Tan (Vietnam).

Major cooperation projects in the Mekong countries proceed smoothly. Currently, there are numerous capacity cooperation projects among the Mekong countries, including many infrastructure demonstration projects: the China–Laos Railway, and the China–Thailand Railway, etc.

There are also pilot projects in energy cooperation: the Hai Duong Coal-fired Power Plant in Vietnam, the China–Laos Nam Ou River Cascade Hydropower Project, the Nangpai Hydropower Project, etc. In the manufacturing sector, there are the China–Cambodia Preah Vihear Sugar Mill, the China–Myanmar Cement Factory, etc. There are demonstrative projects of agricultural cooperation: the China-Cambodia Ecological Agriculture Comprehensive Development Project, the China–Myanmar Agricultural Cooperation Project, etc. Three China-sponsored economic zones are under smooth construction: the Sihanoukville Special Economic Zone in Cambodia, the Seseta Integrated Development Zone in Vientiane, Laos, and the Long Jiang Industrial Park in Vietnam. Plus, the China–Vietnam (Shenzhen–Haiphong) Economic and Trade Cooperation Park (VCEP) and the Thai–Chinese Rayong Industrial Zone (TCR) are also underway, providing an opportunity for Chinese enterprises to expand their investment in the Mekong countries. In addition, the Kyaukpyu Special Economic Zone in Myanmar is also under preparation. Nearly 30 large-scale projects have been carried out in the Mekong countries, including the construction of railroads, highways, hydropower stations, and economic development zones. Especially after the completion of the China–Laos Railway, a large amount of imported and exported goods have been shuttled among the different countries.

In recent years, the production capacity cooperation conducted by the LMC has had an outstanding performance in the textile industry. In 2020, the Fifth LMC Foreign Ministers' Meeting was held in Vientiane. At the meeting, the six ministers reviewed the achievements of the Second Leaders' Meeting and the Fourth Foreign Ministers' Meeting of the LMC. After discussing production capacity cooperation, Article 9 of the Joint Press Communiqué of the Fifth Foreign Ministers' Meeting was issued. The foreign ministers supported optimizing the distribution of the regional production capacity in accordance with the Joint Declaration on Production Capacity Cooperation among the Lancang-Mekong countries, exchanging complementary production capacity advantages and enhancing the countries' position in the global and industrial value chains. The ministers noted the progress made in the establishment of the Production Capacity and Investment Cooperation Alliance and the launch of the "Multi-parks in Multi-countries" project, as well as the First LMC Summit of the Textile Industry, organized by the business associations of the six countries. Joint Declaration on Production Capacity Cooperation in the Textile and Garment Industry among Lancang-Mekong Countries was released after the summit.

China's textile industry has responded positively to the LMC mechanism and has taken the lead in organizing international production capacity cooperation in the textile and garment industry in the Mekong Basin. The fruits of the Lancang-Mekong textile industry were prominently showcased at the highly regarded Milan Fashion Week, where the products made a significant impact.

The Nam Ou 7 Hydropower Station in Laos

On December 25, 2023, the Five-Year Plan of Action on Cross-Border Economic Cooperation of Lancang-Mekong Countries was issued, which once again made it clear that LMC is an innovative sub-regional cooperation mechanism for the basin countries to build and share through joint consultation and sharing, and identified connectivity, production capacity, cross-border economic cooperation, water resources, agriculture, and poverty alleviation as the five key areas of cooperation.

Guided by the philosophy of mutual help, and upgraded production capacities as the cornerstone of development, the production capacity cooperation of the Lancang-Mekong countries has been progressing constantly. All participating countries exchange complementary advantages and jointly promote the rapid and high-quality development of production capacity.

Effective Cooperation to Upgrade Production Capacity

Like a beautiful ink painting completed with free strokes, since its inception, the cooperation on production capacity among the six Lancang-Mekong countries has embodied the reaching of continuous consensuses that respect differences, which is the essence of the LMC.

The cooperation on production capacity constitutes the content of the painting, and the framework of cooperation is like the piece of ink-splashed rice paper, which outlines the general direction for the cooperation.

By means of cooperation on production capacity, the related infrastructure facilities of the Lancang-Mekong countries include transportation, power and energy facilities, and their comprehensive service capabilities can be significantly improved, thereby removing the biggest obstacles that hinder the rapid economic development of these countries, and bringing their economy to a stage of achieving significant growth.

A typical feature of the cooperation on production capacity among the Lancang-Mekong countries is the so-called "multi-nation multi-park" mode. At present, the cooperation on production capacity mainly takes the form of overseas economic cooperation zones and cross-border economic cooperation zones. Industrial parks, such as economic cooperation zones, accommodate international development projects, facilitate industrial agglomeration, and help reduce production costs when an industry develops to a certain scale. Apart from this, the construction of industrial parks can also reduce the risks that enterprises may encounter during international cooperation on production capacity and can also facilitate cooperative management.

Driven by the LMC, a spatial layout of China's international cooperation industrial parks has been completed, which involves the deployment of port parks along the Lancang-Mekong River, industrial parks, and international ports in node cities along the Southeast Asian section of the Trans-Asian Railway network, cross-border economic cooperation zones and bordered economic cooperation zones along key ports on the border, port economic cooperation zones along important ports on the banks of the Indian Ocean and the Pacific Ocean, and agricultural demonstration zones and cross-border tourism pilot zones along the comprehensive transportation lines.

Six major cross-border economic cooperation zones have been completed and put into operation in the six countries, namely, the Pingxiang (China)-Dong Dang (Vietnam) Cross-Border Economic Cooperation Zone, the Dongxing (China)-Mong Cai (Vietnam) Cross-Border Economic Cooperation Zone, the Longbang (China)-Tra Linh (Vietnam) Cross-Border Economic Cooperation Zone, the Hekou (China)-Lao Cai (Vietnam) Cross-Border Economic Cooperation Zone, the Mohan (China)-Boten (Laos) Cross-Border Economic Cooperation Zone, and the Ruili (China)-Muse (Myanmar) Cross-Border Economic Cooperation Zone.

At present, international cooperation on production capacity among the Lancang-Mekong countries includes projects developed by a joint venture supported and established by governments of two countries (e.g., the Vientiane SDZ in Laos), projects led by enterprises and supported by governments (e.g., the Thai-Chinese Rayong Industrial Zone), projects led and planned by governments (e.g., the six cross-border economic cooperation zones established by China and the other five Mekong countries), projects led by governments and promoted by enterprises and the market mechanism (e.g., the Sihanoukville Special Economic Zone in Cambodia), projects led by governments and joint promoted by multinational enterprise groups (e.g., the Kyaukpyu Special Economic Zone in Myanmar), and projects independently invested and developed by enterprises (e.g., the Longjiang Industrial Park in Vietnam).

With the proceeding of the LMC mechanism, cooperation projects among countries have yielded fruitful results, particularly in areas such as high-end manufacturing and commodity trade, which seemed far away from our daily lives, making it difficult for us to intuitively feel the actual benefits. The fruit industry, however, is one of the highlights of LMC that deserves special attention, where international exchanges and cooperation have been strengthened with the help of LMC, bringing more fruit options and better consumption experience to the people of the basin countries, which vividly epitomizes the LMC in real life. Fruits are an important agricultural product and a major trade category in the

A fruit market in Siem Reap

Lancang-Mekong region. Strengthening cooperation in the fruit industry among the Lancang-Mekong countries will not only bring more varieties to the "fruit plates" of people from China, Thailand, Cambodia, Laos, Myanmar, and Vietnam but will also help strengthen regional cooperation in agriculture and trade among these countries, promote industrial development of the local regions, and help the local fruit farmers greatly increase their income and even become rich.

To celebrate the progress made in the fruit trade under LMC, the Lancang-Mekong Fruit Festival has been organized annually since 2021. The Project Roadshow session of the 2023 Greater Mekong Subregion Economic Corridor Governors' Forum and Lancang-Meikong Fruit Festival was held at Haigeng Convention Center, Yunnan Province. Fruit industry enterprises from home and abroad gathered together to promote their projects and signed six projects on the spot to help the fruit industry develop.

In the first quarter of 2023, China's fruit trade with the Mekong countries reached US$1.747 billion. Thailand is the most important market for China's imports of fruits and fruit products: China's total fruit imports from Thailand amounted to US$5.076 billion from January to July 2023, a 10.65% increase year-on-year. Among them, durian is the main category of fruits imported by China from Thailand, which accounts for 95% of all imported durian in China. In addition, Thailand sits atop China's imported green coconut volume, reaching 523,000 tons. From January to July 2023, Myanmar exported more than 40,000 tons of watermelon to China through Wanding Port, generating US$28.697 million in foreign exchange.

What was more, upon the opening of the entire line of the China–Laos Railway on December 3, 2022, a train carrying fruits from Thailand and Laos departed from the designated monitoring site for imported fruits at the Mohan Railway Port in Yunnan to the Mohan Station of the China–Laos Railway. As the first direct train carrying imported fruits that ran on the China–Laos Railway, it carried the first batch of imported fruits that were transported by railway throughout the process to all parts of China. With 25 containers, the train carried 351 tons of Lao bananas, 154 tons of Thai longan, and 38 tons of durians, totaling 543 tons.

These fruits departed from Vientiane, Laos, and arrived at the Mohan Port via the "Friendship Tunnel" located on the border between China and Laos.

During this event, Wei Zhenglin, deputy director of the International Cooperation Department of the Ministry of Agriculture and Rural Affairs, said that "fruit has been an important agricultural product and a major trade category for the Lancang-Mekong region. The Lancang-Mekong Fruit Festival aims to adhere to the principle of the LMC; that is, 'a pragmatic and efficient model that prioritizes development,' so as to share development opportunities, strengthen the cooperation on fruit and other agricultural industries in the Greater Mekong Subregion, and promote mutual benefit among the participating countries."

China is one of the largest fruit exporters among the six Lancang-Mekong countries. In addition, the LMC makes it possible for fruit products to circulate among the member countries. For example, Cambodia is an important producer of mangoes, longans, carambolas, and other fruits. According to a report released by the Ministry of Agriculture, Forestry and Fisheries of Cambodia, in 2022, Cambodia exported a total of 265,229.76 tons of mangoes and mango products. Among them, fresh mangoes accounted for 91.42%, totaling 242,483.76 tons, marking a 148.38% increase over 2020. Vietnam was the top buyer of fresh Cambodian mangoes in 2021, with a purchase volume of 199,077.38 tons, followed by Thailand (38,419.28 tons).

Cooperation among the Lancang-Mekong countries has exhibited a positive trend, which draws a grand blueprint for the future development of these countries that is bound to produce desired results. At the First Lancang-Mekong Fruit Festival, Pathumwadee Imtour, minister-counselor of the Thai Embassy in China, said in her speech that as one of the most dynamic emerging cooperation mechanisms in the Greater Mekong Subregion, the LMC serves as an important cooperative framework for the six member countries to sharpen their competitive advantages, drive their economic growth, and promote sustainable development. She continued that, focusing on mutual benefit, the LMC has yielded fruitful results in improving the varieties of agricultural products, improving the production skills of farmers, and promoting the trade of agricultural products. She further stated that Thailand will continue to strengthen its cooperation with China to bring more Thai tropical fruits to the Chinese market.

At present, various fruit deep-processing industry chains are becoming increasingly developed. The LMC has made it possible for more and more people to taste the "weird" processed fruit products that have high quality from other Lancang-Mekong countries, including jams, juices, dried fruits, fruit cakes, etc.

On December 3, 2021, the China–Laos Railway officially opened for operation. Starting from Kunming, China in the north, to Vientiane, Laos in the south, the "steel giant" brings "sweet" benefits that are so soft and so refreshing to the people living in the Lancang-Mekong region with its strong arms.

During the Fruit Festival, fruit stores from thousands of companies in more than 100 cities across China launched LMC fruit promotion campaigns aimed to further promote fruit transactions and meet the demand of the local people. Yu Huiyong, chairman of Shenzhen Pagoda Industrial (Group) Co., Ltd., said that the Lancang-Mekong Fruit Festival provides an excellent opportunity for enterprises to seek additional investment and trade cooperation. He hoped to take this opportunity to strengthen the cooperation between Pagoda and the Mekong countries in the whole fruit industry chain, including fruit production, processing, distribution, etc., to drive the economic development of the local region with the fruit industry, and to help promote the LMC in the agricultural industry.

Cooperation in production capacity among the Lancang-Mekong countries has brought about rapid economic development and increased trade among these countries, with the fruit industry as a prominent example. Nowadays, in fruit stores, when consumers purchase previously expensive fruits imported from other Lancang-Mekong countries, they can get subsidies and thus enjoy prices that are generally lower than market prices. This is especially the case after the China–Laos Railway opened. To take durian as an example, in cities like Kunming, the price of in-season durian can be as low as RMB 38 to 48 per kilogram.

The durian picking season in Thailand begins in May every year. The practice of durian planting in Thailand can be traced back to more than 100 years ago. Now, more than 200 varieties of durian are produced in this country. Thailand has become the largest fresh durian importer in the world, with more than 80% of its durian exported to China.

Whether in Thailand, the origin of the fruit, or in China, the importing country, durian has always been a luxury with a relatively high price compared with other fruits. However, to some extent, the cooperation on production capacity among the Lancang-Mekong countries has helped to lower the price, bringing the people from the two countries to realize their "freedom in their choice of fruit."

Now, the cooperation regarding production capacity among the Lancang-Mekong countries is moving into a phase of focusing on larger production scales. However, rapid development also brings about technical problems regarding the industrial assembly line. To solve the problems, the six countries have insisted upon frequent communications and mutual assistance. Taking Cambodia as an example, starting from the end of 2021, China Certification and Inspection Traceability coordinated its domestic and foreign resources to launch a Fruit Quality

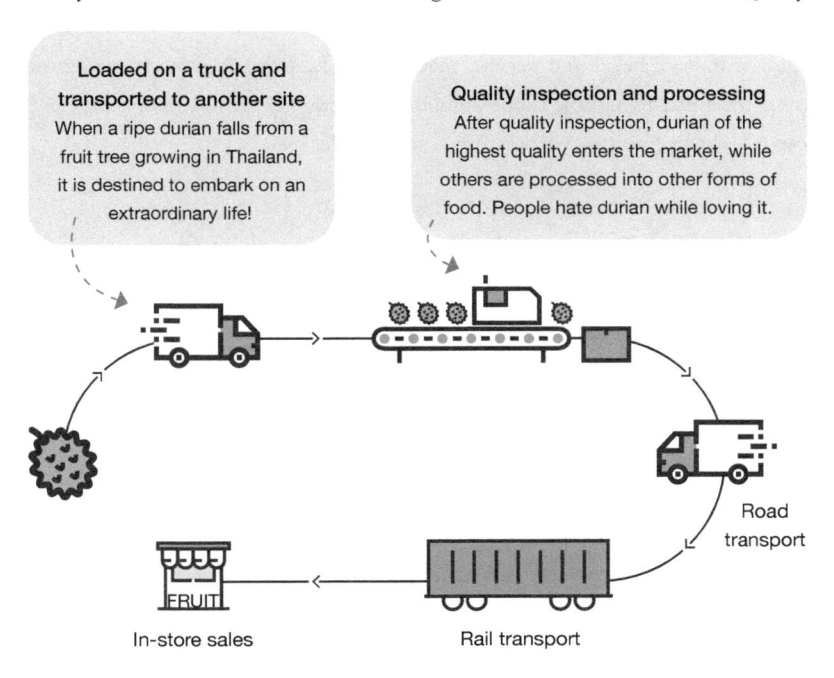

Loaded on a truck and transported to another site
When a ripe durian falls from a fruit tree growing in Thailand, it is destined to embark on an extraordinary life!

Quality inspection and processing
After quality inspection, durian of the highest quality enters the market, while others are processed into other forms of food. People hate durian while loving it.

Road transport

In-store sales   Rail transport

The journey of durian

Assurance Project in Cambodia, which standardized its fruit production. All fruits that are picked from trees planted in the Lancang-Mekong Quality Demonstration Orchards have to go through customs and logistics procedures before they finally flow into the market.

Since 2016, based on full consultation, the six countries have put forward 12 measures that they can jointly take to enhance their cooperation on production capacity. The 12 measures do not only represent a consensus, but also serve as a guarantee for the governments and the people from the six countries.

As a result of the cooperation on production capacity among the Lancang-Mekong countries, successive achievements have been accomplished in areas such as electricity, fruit, processing, and spare parts. Such achievements, like the Nam Ou River Hydropower Station, have been continuously powering the participating countries.

In the final analysis, every effort is for the people's livelihoods, aiming to ensure that the people of all participating countries enjoy a life of better quality. Only with such belief and perseverance can the Lancang-Mekong model grow more dynamically, and the cooperation on production capacities among the Lancang-Mekong countries becomes more sustainable.

Cooperation on production capacity among the Lancang-Mekong countries

o Opportunities for international cooperation on production capacity among the six countries

All six countries are faced with challenges in terms of their infrastructure construction, improving their industrial structures, and the pursuit of sustainable economic and social development. However, currently, the process of industrialization and urbanization is accelerating, the adjustment of industrial structures are intensifying, and the infrastructure connectivity among the six countries is constantly advancing, all of which bring great opportunities for possible international cooperation on production capacity among the six countries.

○ **Further promoting cooperation among the Lancang-Mekong countries**

Considering the rapid and substantial development that has been achieved in economic exchanges among the six countries, and the close economic cooperative partnership that has been formed, the heads of state/government of the six countries agreed to further promote cooperation among them.

○ **Protecting the environment and the natural resources**

Cooperation on production capacity among the six countries should be conducted on the condition that sustainable development is ensured, and considerations are given to protecting the environment and natural resources.

○ **Bringing about good economic and social benefits**

Cooperation on production capacity among the six countries should focus on the joint promotion of economic development and industrial transformation of the relevant countries. Such collaborations can be attained by hiring more local staff and procuring more local materials. Local people can be trained into qualified corporate staff, so that the employment rate of the local region can be increased, good economic and social benefits can be produced, and necessary support can be provided for the development of small and medium-sized enterprises during their production processes.

○ **Transforming potential in cooperation into sustained results**

All participating countries should strengthen their exchange of experience and expertise in terms of the formulation of macroeconomic policies and industrial development strategies, collaborate to enlarge human resources, promote innovation and transfer advanced technologies, complement each other in their competitive advantages, and dock their respective development needs, so as to transform their potential in cooperation into sustained results.

○ **Creating a good business environment**

The six countries should be encouraged to cooperate on production capacity in the gold industry and financial institutions, and consider the market demand, the commercial principles and the international practices, for the purpose of achieving win-win results. At the same time, governments of the six countries should be committed to maintaining a stable and sustainable macroeconomic environment, creating a good business environment, promoting orderly and free flowing economic factors, develop strategies so that resources are allocated in a highly efficient way, allowing for the deep integration of markets, strengthening communications and the coordination of policies among them, so as to create favorable conditions for cooperation on production capacity among these countries.

○ Continuously expand cooperative areas and improve the quality of cooperation

Priority should be given to the promotion of cooperation on production capacity in electrical power, power grids, automobiles, metallurgy, building materials, supporting industries, the light and textile industries, medical equipment, information communication, rail transit, waterway transportation, air transportation, equipment manufacturing, renewable energy, agriculture, agricultural and aquatic product processing, etc., in accordance with the legal environment and developmental reality of relevant countries, and by relying on existing platforms for transportation connectivity and industrial agglomeration areas. The six countries will work together to promote progress in cooperation on major projects that meet the development needs of each country, continuously expand the areas of cooperation, and improve the quality of cooperation.

○ Bringing the results of cooperation on production capacity to benefit the people from all six countries

Cooperation on production capacity among the six countries will further consolidate the already close economic ties among them. Through their cooperation on production capacity, the participating countries should share opportunities, meet challenges, and achieve sustainable development and common prosperity, so as to manifest the results of cooperation to benefit the people from all the participating countries.

○ Making full use of existing bilateral and multilateral financial resources

The six countries should make full use of existing bilateral and multilateral financial resources including the Asian Infrastructure Investment Bank to support their cooperation on production capacity, and continuously explore other available financial resources for the same purpose.

- ○ The principles of mutual benefit, equality, and achieving win-win results

  Cooperation on production capacity among the six countries should be based on the principles of mutual benefit, equality, and achieving win-win results, and governed by the domestic laws of each country, as well as international treaties and agreements to which all of the six countries are party to.

- ○ Improving the capacity to achieve sustainable development of the participating countries

  Cooperation on production capacity serves as an important means to promote the LMC, which is conductive to optimizing the distribution of the regional production capacity, raising the status of the participating countries in the global value chain, and improving the sustainable development capabilities of the participating countries.

- ○ Promoting regional cooperation on trade and investment

  The purpose of cooperation on production capacity among the six countries is to promote cooperation regarding regional trade and investment, as well as the capacity for industrial development of the six countries, by making full use of their competitive advantages, manufacturing capabilities and market size, through the use of various methods such as direct investment, project contracting, technical cooperation, and the importing and exporting of equipment.

Green Production Capacity Relying on Lucid Waters and Lush Mountains

The Lancang-Mekong region boasts a beautiful environment, a pleasant climate, and a large number of species. The mountains are as green as emeralds, the rivers stretch miles long, and there are birds and monkeys chattering throughout the day. The seasons are distinct with different kinds of scenery, and the climate varies every several miles.

The key areas of international cooperation on production capacity among the Lancang-Mekong countries include transportation infrastructure construction, mineral resources, hydropower resources, new energy, manufacturing, biological planting, processing, etc., most of which rely on natural resources. However, rapid industrial development exerts an inevitable impact on the environment, and currently, the six countries are facing uncertain challenges brought about by climate change. Therefore, it is urgent for them to further strengthen their cooperation regarding the construction of regional sustainable infrastructure. As a prompt action to address the issue, countries located in the Lancang-Mekong Basin established a Lancang-Mekong Environmental Cooperation Center, and the year 2022 marks the fifth anniversary of the establishment of the center. Since the establishment of the center, various conferences and seminars have been held to come up with suggestions regarding solving current environmental problems and ensuring adequate production capacities in the Lancang-Mekong region.

Building a green Lancang-Mekong region has been another goal that all six countries have been pursuing, in addition to the target to develop their industrial production capacity. The Mekong countries should work together not only to produce "valuable assets" of high production capacity, but also to guard our "lucid waters and lush mountains." The Green Lancang-Mekong Initiative proposed by the six countries symbolizes their practice of guarding a green Lancang-Mekong region. As a flagship project for the implementation of the LMC, the initiative aims to promote the sustainable development of the six countries in the sub-region and promote cooperation in ecological and environmental protection in the Lancang-Mekong region; provide a platform for dialogue on environmental and development policies among the countries in the sub-region, so as to enhance their environmental governance capabilities; and strengthen cooperation on constructing capabilities for countries in the region. It consists of five major parts, i.e., Lancang-Mekong environmental policy dialogues, the mainstreaming of Lancang-Mekong environmental policies, Lancang-Mekong environmental capacity building, demonstration cooperation on the environment of the Lancang-Mekong region, and the Lancang-Mekong environmental cooperation partnership.

On April 21, 2022, the Green Lancang-Mekong Initiative Lancang-Mekong Roundtable Dialogue on Green, Low-Carbon, and Sustainable Infrastructure was held both online and off-line in Beijing, China. Under the guidance of the Ministry of Ecology and the Environment of the People's Republic of China, the roundtable dialogue was hosted by the Lancang-Mekong Environmental Cooperation Center / Foreign Environmental Cooperation Center of the Ministry of Ecology and Environment of China and was co-organized by the World Resources Institute, the World Wildlife Fund, the Wildlife Conservation Society, Oxfam, the Asia Foundation, and Conservation International. Nearly 300 delegates from the Ministry of Ecology and Environment and local ecological and environmental departments of China, climate and environment departments from the other Mekong countries, agencies of the United Nations in China, and relevant international organizations, research institutions and enterprises, attended the meeting. Delegates from various countries and institutions conducted friendly exchanges, cordial dialogues, and joint discussions, making suggestions and exploring the goals, methods, and prospects of the green development of the Lancang-Mekong region in the future.

In 2021, at the Sixth LMC Foreign Ministers' Meeting, the Joint Statement on Enhancing Sustainable Development Cooperation of the Lancang-Mekong Countries was released, aiming to promote the creation of an environmentally friendly and innovation-driven economic growth model and helping the region complete a better, greener, and smarter post-pandemic recovery. "Building a green Lancang-Mekong region" is the focus, and sustainable cooperation and sustainable infrastructure construction are indispensable in terms of the transformation of and cooperation on production capacity among the Lancang-Mekong countries at this stage.

Many experts believe that the way to help the Lancang-Mekong countries build climate-resilient infrastructure, adjust production capacity development methods, and deepen environmental cooperation starts with various aspects such as capital investment, knowledge sharing, and project demonstrations.

As a very important interdisciplinary science topic, the environment is actually closely related to development issues. It now mainly involves three core areas, i.e., coping with global climate change, conserving biodiversity, and dealing with marine litter. In terms of capital investment, the participating countries should allocate more funding for green energy technological development and support the transformation of various industries toward a green development model.

All participating countries should conduct strategic cooperation, sharing new technologies and methods that relate to achieving low-carbon emissions and sustainable green development, and provide technical assistance to each other so that they can benefit from extensive communication and sharing. The joint statement issued by the foreign ministers from the six countries in 2021 included the joint construction of a Lancang-Mekong Knowledge Hub for Low-Carbon, Green, and Sustainable Infrastructure in its key agenda for the next stage of development. It means that in the future when the six countries communicate and share products with each other, they need to continuously put environmental issues high on the agenda and try to solve environmental problems that may come with an increase in production and construction. To effectively cope with the above issue, the six countries can mainly start with the construction of leading, demonstration, and model projects.

In recent years, the construction of LMC low-carbon industrial parks has become a hot topic among governments and experts from various participating countries. Among them, the construction of sustainable industrial community projects in the Guangxi Zhuang Autonomous Region constitutes a typical case for green Lancang-Mekong governance. Taking the Jiangnan Comprehensive Manufacturing Development Zone in Guigang, Guangxi, as an example, relying on rich agricultural and forestry resources and using forestry waste as fuel, a biomass cogeneration project was built to achieve the goal of having full coverage of central heating in the zone. By replacing coal with agricultural and forestry biomass energy, on the one hand, carbon emissions were reduced, clean heating was achieved, and the environment in the rural areas was improved; on the other hand, the possibilities for green employment and wealth accumulation were increased, and huge comprehensive social, economic, and environmental benefits were obtained.

China has signed cooperation documents with Myanmar, Laos, Cambodia, and other countries in terms of the offer it has made that relates to the provision of environmental monitoring equipment and solar photovoltaic power generation systems to these countries. Other projects aimed at enhancing the capacities of the Mekong countries in dealing with climate change include the joint construction of the Vientiane Saysettha Low-Carbon Demonstration Zone by China and Laos. The continued development of such systems and industrial models can bring about constant optimization of equipment, high-quality sharing based on connectivity and communication, and the development of production capacities for the six countries. All of these contribute to the building of a green production capacity and the formation of a green Lancang-Mekong framework.

The year 2022 marks the successful completion of the First Five-Year Plan of Action on the LMC. The end of one phase means the beginning of another. On December 25, 2023, the Five-Year Plan of Action on Lancang-Mekong Cooperation (2023–2027) was officially released, in which the key directions of production capacity cooperation were specially clarified. In the future, the role of the Joint Working Group on Capacity Cooperation among Lancang-Mekong Countries will be given full play, and a Three-Year Plan of Action on LMC Production Capacity and Investment Cooperation among Lancang-Mekong Countries will be formulated to optimize the layout of regional production capacity and promote the production capacity cooperation to achieve green growth.

The enhanced development of production capacity for the Lancang-Mekong region depends on lucid waters and lush mountains, and like the everlasting waters and the mountains in the region, the friendship among the Lancang-Mekong countries will last forever.

Working Together to Upgrade Production Capacity

The Lancang-Mekong production capacity cooperation is like a big family. In this family, we live and work together, and everyone contributes to building this family. There is also a sweet warmth under all kinds of affections. In the process of production capacity cooperation and development, more and more industrial projects have emerged, especially because of increasingly improved infrastructure construction. People in the Lancang-Mekong countries have taken this opportunity to communicate and find new platforms to support their own development.

Production capacity cooperation among the Lancang-Mekong countries has created a lot of jobs and brought us many warm stories. As mentioned above, the textile industry is a prominent area in production capacity cooperation among the Lancang-Mekong countries, and the costumes in these countries have both different customs and similar characteristics.

At the beginning of 2020, in the production workshop of the Myanmar Light Hat Industry (Ruili) Co., Ltd., located in Dehong Dai and Jingpo Autonomous Prefecture, Yunnan Province, people can hear the warm and lively sound of Myanmar pop songs. Taking a closer look, there were more than 200 Myanmar workers who were busy on the assembly line. One of them is 24-year-old Tin Ya Wu from Myanmar, who has been working here for seven months and now earns nearly 400,000 kyat a month. "This is my first time in China, and the factory is very respectful of our customs. Our friends from the village said they wanted to work here as well when they knew how well we were doing here." Tin Ya Wu said. There are many people like her in the workshop, who are bending their heads and doing the work carefully.

Tin Ya Wu's sense of gaining is only a microcosm of the benefits of the China-Myanmar cross-border production capacity cooperation. With the steady progress that is being made in the LMC, more and more individuals and enterprises can benefit from it, and more and more people can achieve their own values in the production capacity cooperative project.

On November 21, 2019, the First Myanmar (Lashio) China (Lincang) Border Economic and Trade Fair (hereinafter referred to as the "Border Trade Fair"), co-hosted by China and Myanmar, took place in Lashio, Myanmar. The wide variety of high-quality products attracted a large number of Myanmar enterprises and local people to visit the exhibition.

"Come and have a taste of our Myanmar pastry!" said the founder of Myanmar Hani pastry, Madan Dan, as he warmly greeted customers. As the best-selling product at this trade fair, Hanni Crispy Rolls has settled on an agreement of intention to cooperate with two companies in Lincang, China. "The Border Trade Fair held in Lashio has brought new opportunities for the development of small and medium-sized enterprises in Myanmar." Madan Dan is confident in the development of his business.

The Myanmar College Students Pioneer Park in Lincang Bianhe District has officially opened, providing Myanmar entrepreneurs with low start-up costs and better opportunities. The construction of overseas parks in Mandalay, including Myitkyina Industrial Park and Myuda Baoshan Industrial Park is progressing smoothly. In August 2019, the China (Yunnan) Pilot Free Trade Zone was officially established, bringing convenience to more China-Myanmar cooperation.

"Today is the happiest day since I started working in Ruili. I received the official establishment of the First (Yunnan) Pilot Free Trade Zone, which issued a lot of 'Pakpo Cards.'" Wu Ang Sanlin, a Burmese migrant worker who has been working in Ruili City, Dehong Prefecture, for two years, is overjoyed after receiving a Pakpo Card on May 29, 2020. The China (Yunnan) Pilot Free Trade Zone held an opening ceremony for the Pakpo Card on Wednesday, and more than 100 Burmese working in Ruili City received the cards.

The Pakpo Card is a combination of a "Myanmar National Identity Card," a "Myanmar-China Border Pass," a "Health Certificate," a "Work Permit," a "Temporary Residence Permit for Overseas Border Residents in Yunnan Province," and a "Training Certificate." Shao Yongbao, a director of the Ruili Foreign Personnel Service Management Center, said that with the Pakpo Card, foreigners in Ruili can enjoy several services and benefits, including accommodation, renting, employment, travel, medical treatment, and communications, which will completely change the situation of Myanmar people when facing local affairs, communication and travel dilemmas that have occurred in the past.

Whether it is Tin Ya Wu's sense of gaining, the intimate feeling of the Pakpo Card, or the sense of hope provided by the entrepreneurial park, these are all refreshing and warm feelings brought on by production capacity cooperation.

These heart-warming stories prove that the Lancang-Mekong region is a big family, living under the same roof and pulling and pushing each other from behind. Such powers may not be overwhelming or earth-shaking, but they are reflected in every little thing. The same goes for production capacity cooperation. The original purpose of such cooperation is human development. Later, it brought about better lives and more hope for people in the Lancang-Mekong region.

As long as the six countries continue to work together for the people and think in the same direction, the future of production capacity cooperation in the Lancang-Mekong region will be bright and full of positive energy.

The Abundant Lancang-Mekong River and the Busy Cross-Border Trade

The Lancang-Mekong River nourishes the people of the six countries—China, Myanmar, Laos, Thailand, Cambodia, and Vietnam. It covers an area of 810,000 square kilometers and nearly 300 million people live on this rich and beautiful land. Since ancient times, in this land, there have been a lot of merchants who have come from all directions with busy business dealings and the sounding of carriage bells.

During the Song Dynasty (AD 960–1279), the Bagan Dynasty of Burma presented white elephants, spices, and other rare treasures to Dali on several occasions, which were recorded in Chinese historical books such as the *History of Song*, *Zhu Fan Zhi* (*Records of Foreign People*), *Nanzhao's Unofficial History*, and the *Donghua Records*. After the Yuan and Ming dynasties, Yunnan merchants moved to Siam, Myanmar, and other countries and brought local gems, cotton, and millet back to Yunnan. By the start of the Qing Dynasty (AD 1616–1911), there were more than ten trade routes in Yunnan. In the 21st century, building a more dynamic platform based on long-standing commercial ties and bridging the common aspirations of the people in the six countries is an important driving force for achieving prosperity along the Lancang-Mekong River.

Forge Ahead with Confidence

In recent years, LMC has not only developed rapidly and achieved remarkable results, but it has also won praise from all over the world. In practice, the Lancang-Mekong Cooperative mechanism has become an effective platform for China to extensively explore and advance South-South cooperation. It has become the first concrete action in the world to take the lead in responding to the Post-2015 Development Agenda that was proposed by the UN Development Summit.

The Lancang-Mekong Business Council

In order to promote economic development in the Lancang-Mekong River region and further strengthen exchanges and practical cooperation among the business communities of countries in the region, the Lancang-Mekong Business Council was jointly initiated by the China Council for the Promotion of International Trade and Mekong countries in March 2018 as a part of the LMC. The members mainly include the Chinese Council for the Promotion of International Trade, the Greater Mekong Business Council, the Cambodian General Chamber of Commerce, the Laos National Chamber of Commerce and Industry, the Myanmar Chamber of Commerce and Industry, the Thailand Chamber of Commerce and Industry and the Vietnam Chamber of Commerce and Industry. To promote the development of the Lancang-Mekong Business Council, the Chinese Council for the Promotion of International Trade was the first to establish the Chinese Committee of the Lancang-Mekong Business Council. The Lancang-Mekong Business Council plays an important leading role in promoting bilateral partnerships and achieving common prosperity in the region. In particular, it has become an important bond for bringing all parties together in trade and investment promotion activities, such as international trade and investment fairs, exhibitions, road shows, and enterprise docking.

The LMC Expo

The LMC Expo will focus on trade and investment, cultural tourism, sales of specialty commodities, and cross-border talent exchanges and serve as a stage for the Lancang-Mekong countries to "show and promote themselves." Many high-quality products and high-end talents have been favored, which is like the "horse" finally being admired by its "Bole."

From November 15 to 20, 2006, the First Lancang-Mekong Subregion National Commodity Expo was held at Kunming Dianchi International Convention and Exhibition Center. With the theme of "drinking from the same river for common development," and focusing on promoting the construction of the "Belt and Road," the conference actively integrated important elements such as the "Southern Ancient Silk Road" and the "Ancient Tea Horse Road," and promoted economic and trade negotiations and cooperation among the countries in the Lancang-Mekong sub-region. It was an important foundation project for the construction of the Lancang-Mekong cooperation mechanism. At the Expo, for the first time in China, 400 Thai OTOP (one village, one product) merchants were invited to build a Thai-themed exhibition with prominent Thai characteristics, hold Thai commodity promotion activities with unique Thai customs, and create a simple and authentic Thai cultural feast. It is worth mentioning that the highlight of this Expo was also the Dianchi Music Festival, which was held at the same time. The music festival took "The Pearl of the Plateau" as its theme and created a cultural exchange platform for LMC. The International High-end Health Forum was also held during the exhibition, and international exchanges in the fields of health and leisure were carried out, which adhered to the concept of health care in the 21st century. At the same time, the provincial government of Yunnan also led teams to promote the Expo internationally in the form of promotion meetings in Penang, Malaysia, Vientiane, Laos, and Bangkok, Thailand.

From November 24 to 29, 2007, the Second Lancang-Mekong Sub-Region Commodity Expo and Lancang-Mekong Dianchi Forum was held in Kunming Dianchi Convention and Exhibition Center. The theme of the forum was "Jointly Discussing New Measures and Building New Mechanisms for Win-Win Development." The forum mainly focused on "cross-border trade facilitation" and "cross-border investment facilitation."

The second Expo consisted of five sections: commodity exhibition, the opening ceremony and themed forum, investment negotiations, mass entrepreneurship and innovation activities, and cultural exchanges and exhibitions. The exhibition area was about 80,000 square meters and had more than 3,000 exhibitors. The exhibition built the Lancang-Mekong National Pavilion, the International Pavilion, the Intangible Cultural Heritage Pavilion, the Health Pavilion, the Automobile Pavilion, the Tourism Pavilion, and the Comprehensive Pavilion, as well as the Special Entrepreneurship and Innovation Pavilion. The establishment of the Mass Entrepreneurship and Innovation Pavilion actively responded to the call for "mass

The Second Lancang-Mekong Sub-Region Commodity Expo

entrepreneurship and innovation" and provided a stage for entrepreneurs and innovative enterprises in the Lancang-Mekong countries.

With the theme of "drinking from the same river for common development," the third Expo was held on November 23, 2018, composed of three parts: the exhibition, the forum, and the conference. "The exhibition" refers to the Expo, which set up seven themed pavilions, including displaying achievements of LMC since the 40th anniversary of reform and opening-up, Lancang-Mekong countries exhibitions, new energy and special commodities, and rosewood and wood art. "The forum" refers to the Third Dianchi Forum of LMC, which, under the theme of "LMC and Regional Economic Integration," promoted the implementation of the Dianchi Declaration from the Second Dianchi Forum of LMC. Covering an area of 55,000 square meters, the exhibition hall has 2,500 booths featuring products not only from the Lancang-Mekong countries but also crafts from Indonesia, cosmetics from South Korea, goods from Malaysia, and cultural artworks from Nepal. The New Energy Hall, which was the largest exhibition area, displayed new energy vehicles, industries, and equipment and attracted many visitors. Cultivating and building new international and regional energy products is a necessary task to

Kunming International Convention and Exhibition Center, hosting the 2019 Lancang-Mekong Cooperation Expo

confront the mass market of energy conservation, the environmental protection industry, and the new energy industry in Southeast Asia.

This year's LMC Expo has also been widely praised by the governments of the Lancang-Mekong countries. Kangzhan Ongsenben, Deputy Minister of Planning and Investment of Laos, said that the LMC Expo is of profound significance and bears witness to friendly relations and further in-depth cooperation among the Lancang-Mekong countries. In the future, Laos will become the logistics center of the Mekong Subregion and will make full use of the platform that stems from the LMC Expo to bring benefits to the Lao and Chinese people. Choon Dala, State Secretary of the Ministry of Commerce of Cambodia, spoke highly of the LMC and the Expo, saying, "We fully support the driving force of LMC to make our trade more international so that it benefits people in the region through cooperation."

Under the theme of "Cross-Border Economic Cooperation and the Pilot Free Trade Zone Development," the 2019 LMC Expo has set up three parallel meetings, namely the China "Double Green" Lancang-Mekong Round Table, the China–Laos Investment Fair, and the China-Cambodia Investment Fair, focusing on "double green" cooperation, namely the green economy and green finance in the Lancang-Mekong region. It also promoted China–Laos and China-Cambodia projects, and contracts were signed that were worth about RMB 1.3 billion and will yield fruitful results. In addition, activities were held to promote the Lancang-Mekong Expo Forum to enter Yunnan Province and the China (Yunnan) Pilot Free Trade Zone. The main examples were Youlian Group and Honghe University, which signed the cooperation agreement on jointly building the "China-Cambodia Cultural Innovation and Entrepreneurship Center" and held the opening ceremony for the center. A memorandum of cooperation was signed between PLOYGREENLAND of Cambodia and the Shanghai Qi Chi Investment Management Co., Ltd. At the same time, it has also set up professional sections such as free trade and investment, cross-border entrepreneurship for international talents, and cross-border investment, which covers the field of "international talents."

Create Wealth with Good Strategies

A Long Way to Go Higher

Today's LMC is in its prime, growing like a towering tree. Despite the impact of the COVID-19 pandemic on the global economy, trade between China and the five Lancang-Mekong countries in 2021 reached US$398 billion, an increase of 23% and doubling that of 2015.

This is a brilliant achievement. In retrospect, the LMC has witnessed more frequent economic and trade exchanges, which has also promoted mutual trust. The people from the Lancang-Mekong countries are becoming closer to each other. Economic and trade cooperation has brought harmony and prosperity to the people and the governments. In 2022, the trade between China and the other five Mekong countries reached US$416.7 billion. China has become the largest trading partner of Vietnam, Cambodia, Myanmar, and Thailand, the second largest trading partner of Laos, and Vietnam has become the fourth largest trading partner of China. Since 2015, economic growth for the five Mekong countries has exceeded 30%, which is complementary to China's economic development. The five Mekong countries have become important trade partners for China. Steady growth of the regional economy shows strong confidence and the resilience of LMC.

While promoting regional economic development and bringing tangible benefits, the LMC has also been widely praised by the Lancang-Mekong countries. Government officials from some countries have made extremely positive comments on the cooperation, with many of them speaking highly of it.

"So far, Cambodia has benefited from 89 Projects Supported by the LMC Special Fund, with a total value of more than US$20 million, and it has played an important role in promoting the coordinated development of various national undertakings such as water conservancy, agriculture, aviation, education, and culture," said Prak Sokhonn, Cambodia's Deputy Prime Minister and the Minister of Foreign Affairs and International Cooperation.

The Ambassador of Laos for China also spoke highly of the LMC. He said that the current period is the best period in history for the development of Laos-China relations. The two countries will follow the consensus reached by the parties and state leaders of both sides, deepen practical cooperation in trade, agriculture, investment, poverty alleviation, and other fields, and work together to achieve win-win results. The idea of "..." has been deeply rooted in Chinese culture for thousands of years. Since ancient times, Chinese people have always adhered to the concept of neighboring diplomacy, including loving peace, advocating mutual benefits and win-win results, and seeking common ground while respecting differences. Chinese enterprises have actively participated in the construction of the Sihanouk Port Special Economic Zone in Cambodia, the Thai-China Rayong Industrial Park, driving the development of the local textile industry, electronic manufacturing, agriculture, and other fields and broadening cooperation. The investment in the other five Mekong countries has reached new heights, creating a large amount of tax revenue and jobs for local people and achieving mutual benefit and win-win results in a real sense.

Gathering Elites and Sharing Joys and Sorrows

In recent years, owing to the establishment of the LMC platform, Chinese companies have accelerated their investment in the Mekong countries. At the same time, a number of students who have come to China to study have entered such enterprises and become an important part of developing bilateral friendships.

In 2012, Huaxin Cement Co., Ltd. arrived in Cambodia to establish the Huaxin Cambodia Zhuoreding Cement Co., Ltd. Chen Kangliang, an employee of this company, is Cambodian-Chinese. He had dreamed of studying in China since childhood. After graduating from senior high school, he applied for a scholarship from the Yunnan Provincial Government, which helped him embark on the road to study in China, and he studied International Economics and Trade at Yunnan Normal University. During his college years, Chen Kangliang witnessed the development of China, especially Yunnan Province, which benefited him a lot and changed his way of thinking and his philosophy toward life. He had originally chosen to pursue graduate school, but the sudden outbreak of the pandemic put a damper on his plans. Instead of being discouraged, he decided to join the job-hunting army. In 2020, he chose to join Huaxin Cement and was responsible for the sales of key industrial projects. Chen Kangliang, a newcomer to the workplace, was very nervous at the beginning, but the company's unity and love, coupled with support and happiness, reassured him. After working for more than one year, he grew professionally. Because of his confidence and decisiveness and his excellent working performance, he was promoted to be the industrial sales director. In his view, it is commendable that after years of working with employees from both countries, the Chinese employees not only adapted to the local lifestyle but also knew more about the local cultural traditions and customs through cooperation and communication with other Cambodian employees like Chen Kangliang. Some of them can even communicate with the Cambodian employees using simple Cambodian language.

Chen Kangliang, a Chinese-Cambodian

Combining Online and Off-line Methods to Achieve Prosperity

The LMC has brought new prosperity to bilateral trade, which is reflected in the continuous growth of economic and trade areas in recent years, and by also the increasing number of commodities that has resulted in a wide variety coupled with high-quality, in the commercial market. According to Chinese customs statistics, nearly 400 types of agricultural and food products from the Mekong countries have been traded with China, and fruits, vegetables, cereals, aquatic products, nuts, and bird's nests from Lancang-Mekong countries are especially favored by Chinese consumers. It is fair to say that LMC has brought tangible benefits to people from all different backgrounds.

Thailand's "Looking at Me in Chiang Mai" Store project is the epitome of the joint exploration and win-win cooperation between China and relevant countries under the Lancang-Mekong Cooperative mechanism. It is a pilot project that consists of cross-border, e-commerce, and cooperative research under the LMC framework. Led by Chiang Mai University, the store was launched in early 2021, with online sales exceeding 800,000 baht. It has become one of the organizations that provide internship positions so that Chiang Mai University students can learn more about cross-border trade, logistics, product development, and other fields.

The store at Chantai Shopping Mall in Chiang Mai, Thailand, offers a wide range of unique products, such as hand-made handbags that have been woven by villagers in Mae Lam County, volcanic stone dyed cloth from Ubon Province, herbal massage oil from Sukhothai Province, and wood carvings from Nambang Province. It is worth mentioning that the LMC logo is very prominently printed on the promotional posters in the store. In addition to off-line sales, in the corner of the store, several young Thai people make online live broadcasts, shouting enthusiastically. Instantly, the live broadcast room attracted hundreds of customers, sometimes with a daily revenue of tens of thousands of baht. Its booming business is due to the bold exploration of an online sales model. Cha Caiwan, deputy governor of Chiang Mai Prefecture, said that the sales income from the products of the specialty stores would be returned to relevant enterprises, handicraftsmen and villagers, which would become an important source of income for the locals.

Seizing the Rare Opportunity to Step Forward

In recent years, the Mekong countries have developed rapidly and their relations with China have become closer. China has established a community with a shared future with the Mekong countries, and then, the China–Laos, China-Cambodia, and China-Thailand communities that have a shared future have also successively been established. On January 1, 2022, the RCEP came into effect. Covering Cambodia, Laos, Thailand, Vietnam, China, and other countries, the RCEP has the largest population, the largest trade scale, and the greatest potential for development in the world. The member countries of the RCEP account for one-third of the global economic aggregate and will form a large unified market in the future. On this occasion of its seventh anniversary, LMC will have a brighter future and step onto the broad road of achieving common prosperity. This will be the best present for the tenth anniversary of the Belt and Road Initiative.

The land-locked country of Laos is a typical agricultural country with a low level of economic development, and agriculture accounts for 16% of its GDP. However, the trade volume of agricultural products in the country is underperforming, reaching just US$2.42 billion in 2020. As of 2022, China's total merchandise import and export with Laos reached US$5.682 billion, 31% up year-on-year, of which China's imports from Laos were US$3.342 billion, a 25% increase year-on-year. In the future, agricultural products such as sugarcane, bananas, live cattle, cassava, and coffee produced in Laos will become more competitive in the market.

The China–Laos Railway has become a new economic engine for Laos. The Lao government plans to export more agricultural products to China, its largest export destination, through the railway. In 2023, the total import and export freight through the China–Laos Railway increased by 94.91% year-on-year to

4,217,700 tons. Seven hundred and fifty-nine trains have operated on the "Lancang-Mekong Express" for fruits, flowers, and fast-moving consumer goods delivery between Kunming, Yunnan Province, and Vientiane, Laos, with a cumulative cargo value of more than RMB 23 billion.

Cooperative Zones Complementing Each Other

Cross-border economic cooperation refers to a series of cooperative arrangements in the border areas of neighboring countries, which enable the main body of the region to benefit from special industrial, fiscal and tax policies, financial support policies, etc., so that various factors can flow freely across the border and attract factor resources to rapidly concentrate in the border areas. Cross-border economic cooperation combines policies, resources, technologies, talents, and cultures of various countries to achieve the maximum integration of resources and industries, thus promoting the optimal allocation of resources and knowledge. Cross-border economic cooperation can enhance international economic cooperation, promote regional economic development, and enhance local development capacities by strengthening cross-border trade and attracting foreign investment.

China Dongxing-Vietnam's Mong Cai Cross-Border Economic Cooperative Zone

The total planned area of the bilateral core zone is 23.4 square kilometers, of which the Chinese zone covers 9.9 square kilometers and the Vietnamese zone covers 13.5 square kilometers. In order to achieve "opening the first-line to flow freely, and controlling the second-line to efficiently operate," the joint operation area implements the management mode of "two countries and one zone with domestic and foreign customs, free trade, and a closed operation," and also implements the operating mode of "shops being near to factories" in industrial development. From 2015 to 2018, the Cross-Border Economic Cooperative Zone of China Dongxing-Vietnam Mang Street signed a total of 79 cooperative projects with China's large central enterprises, state-owned enterprises, foreign enterprises, and private enterprises, and were worth a total amount of RMB 111.139 billion. The bilateral cooperation has achieved remarkable results. At the same time, China has also built a number of ports, including the only sea-land cold-chain logistics channel that connects Southeast Asian countries, a designated port for grain, a designated port for imported fruit, and the entry port for Thai fruit to enter China through a third country. In the field of financial reform, the cooperative zone has initiated the "Dongxing mode" of having a direct quoted exchange of RMB against the Vietnamese dong and has successively become a pioneer in a number of pilot policies, such as the cross-border two-way transfer of currency and cash between China and Vietnam, and the operation and registration of foreign persons.

Being incorporated into the industrial planning of Fangchenggang City, the Dongxing Cross-Border Economic Cooperation Zone is equipped with good infrastructure and supporting facilities. There are steel and non-ferrous metal industries and two large industrial parks of scale in Fangchenggang City, Qisha, and Southwest Lingang industrial parks. What's more, other industries like energy, grain, oil, and chemical industry are also available.

China and Vietnam take turns to paint the main lines of the Beilun River Bridge every year.

In 2023, Vietnam has planned to set up a pilot Sino-Vietnam Cross-Border Economic Cooperation Zone in Quang Ninh Province. Mong Cai City, the only international port in Vietnam bordering China by land and sea, has great potential for development and is a typical city of border trade. Vietnam has decided to allocate 1,300 hectares of land for a series of infrastructural projects to serve the border trade, which signifies a vigorous momentum for future development.

China Pingxiang-Vietnam Dong Dang Cross-Border Economic Cooperative Zone

The planned construction area of the Chinese side of the cooperative zone reaches 10.2 square kilometers, and the supporting area amounts to 79.42 square kilometers. The operation functions will cover the port operation zone, international logistics zone, bonded processing zone, trade and tourism zone, and the financial and business zone. As a core functional area, the Pingxiang Bonded Zone has become a hot ticket that is being favored by investors. The trade volume of the zone has exceeded RMB 100 billion for several consecutive years, and hundreds of enterprises have settled in the zone, making a series of mutually beneficial and win-win achievements in bonded logistics, bonded processing, cross-border e-commerce and other businesses. Its 2020 annual development performance index has risen by 20 in the country, ranking it first among the four comprehensive protection zones in Guangxi.

The mechanism of "one axis," "two wings," and "two cores" has become the strategic driving model of Chongzuo District, which is known for "opening the door to Vietnam and walking two steps to arrive at ASEAN." According to the development orientation, the overall plan of the Chongzuo Area of China (Guangxi) Pilot Free Trade Zone for 2019–2035 was released, which proposed the functional layout of "one axis, two wings, two cores and multiple clusters." The "one axis" refers to building a comprehensive development axis of the area based on the section from downtown Pingxiang to Youyiguan on the Nanyou

Expressway, connecting various development function units in the area, and scientifically arranging cross-border industries such as cross-border trade, cross-border logistics, cross-border tourism, cross-border finance, and cross-border labor cooperation. The "two wings" refers to the construction of a "five-span" economic belt around the East and the West Road of the comprehensive development axis of the area, and the construction of a cross-border industrial cooperative demonstration zone on the Chinese side. The "two cores" is the key development area planned in Chongzuo District, referring to the comprehensive service core of Pingxiang City in the north, and the business core of cross-border economic cooperation zone in the Youyiguan Port, Puzhai and Nonghuai trading points in the south of the district. The "two cores" complement each other in their respective functions and interact with each other developmentally, which provides growth for Chongzuo District.

China Hekou-Vietnam Lao Cai Cross-Border Economic Cooperative Zone

The cooperative zone is located in an area adjacent to Hekou County, China, and Laojie, Sa Pa County, Vietnam, and it has an advantageous geographical location and favorable natural conditions. The total planned area of the cooperative zone is 21 square kilometers, including 11 square kilometers for the Chinese side and 10 square kilometers for the Vietnamese side. As early as 2013, the People's Government of Yunnan Province issued Several Policies to Support the Construction of the Honghe Estuary Cross-Border Economic Cooperative Zone, which clearly provides encouraging policies and supportive measures in investment, finance, industry, land, customs clearance, and other aspects.

With the promotion of China's Belt and Road Initiative and the construction of Yunnan Province as a main economic center that faces South and Southeast Asia, Hekou has become a transit and distribution center for logistics transportation and inbound and outbound tourism between China and Vietnam and even

ASEAN. In the future, Hekou will become a launching pad for the flow of people, logistics, information, capital, and technology between China and Vietnam, and other ASEAN countries, with a more prosperous future.

In the 1980s, Zeng Wen worked in the Hekou Farm Rubber Factory. He led the factory to work together, plant bamboo forests, and build roads to the factory. In 1992, due to the reform of the farm system, he was transferred to the Hekou Farm Overseas Chinese Border Trade Company. In 2006, he decided to start his own business and set up the Hekou Fangxin Import and Export Co., Ltd. and the Hekou Professional Customs Clearance Company. In his thirties, he began to learn Vietnamese and organized his staff to regularly study the economic dynamics of the national border by understanding the relevant policies of China and Vietnam. Since its establishment, the company has been operating well and developing steadily.

Zeng Wen, whose ancestral home is Huizhou, Guangdong Province, had a grandfather who worked in Malaysia. In the 1950s, his father, Zeng Jinxiu, resolutely returned to China. At that time, China was vigorously developing the rubber industry. As the earliest rubber farm in Yunnan Province, Hekou Farm was the place where many scientists, returned overseas Chinese and young educated people worked, and his father was one of them. Zeng recalled that as a returned overseas Chinese citizen, his father had many choices, but he was willing to devote his life to the rubber industry and gave up the retirement benefits that he could have enjoyed in his later years. The influence of Zeng's father on Zeng Wen continues to this day. Over the past decade, Zeng Wen has organized charitable people to visit rural schools in Hekou on more than ten occasions, and they donated a large number of school supplies. Since 2008, he has also donated more than RMB 300,000 in the name of individuals or companies. After the outbreak of the pandemic, he has made many efforts to donate drinking water, instant noodles, clothes and other supplies and cash to prevention and control areas on 19 occasions, with a total amount of more than RMB 100,000. Zeng Wen's story is the story of the overseas Chinese citizens who return home and their families embracing the world and the populace, as well as the story of struggle and love in the small border town.

China Longbang-Vietnam Tra Linh Cross-Border Economic Cooperative Zone

Longbang Port is the only international national first-class port in Baise City, Guangxi Zhuang Autonomous Region, which integrates roads and railways for trade, tourism, production, and processing. It is one of the more convenient land transportation routes from western Guangxi, eastern Yunnan and southern Guizhou to Vietnam and other Southeast Asian countries. China and Vietnam have actively promoted the joint construction of the China Longbang-Vietnam Chaling Cross-Border Economic Cooperative Zone by issuing the Overall Development Plan of the China Longbang-Vietnam Chaling Cross-Border Economic Cooperative Zone (Chinese Region) (2016–2030). The two sides have achieved fruitful results in infrastructure construction cooperation within the zone. The trade volume of the port's customs clearance in the first year exceeded RMB 100 million, and then maintained an annual growth rate of more than 10%.

In order to smoothly promote the construction of the regional zones in China, the Guangxi Baise Development and Investment Group established a cooperative partnership with Guangxi Jingxi Wansheng Long Investment Co., Ltd at the end of 2015, with an initial investment amount of about RMB 3 billion. Both sides aim to jointly develop, build, and operate the Wansheng Long International Trade and Logistics Center. The center will be built into the core project on the Chinese side of the Cross-Border Economic Cooperative Zone, which has six functional areas, including the Border Trade Zone, the General International Trade Service Zone, the International Multimodal Transit Trade Zone, the International Bonded Processing and Sorting Zone, the ASEAN Free Trade Zone, and the ASEAN Cross-Border E-Commerce Zone.

Vietnam officially issued the plan to build a port economic zone with a total area of 44.56 square kilometers, consisting of Tra Linh Port Park and Kao Ping Park. The first phase of the Tra Linh Port construction includes a port inspection area, storage area, export processing, business center, etc. After completion, it will achieve a seamless connection with the Chinese Longbang Port area. At present,

Chaling's port inspection area, storage area, and passenger inspection channel have been put into use.

China–Laos Mohan-Boten Cross-Border Economic Cooperative Zone

China has become the largest source of investment, the largest export market, and the second largest trading partner of Laos. As the second cross-border economic cooperative zone in China and the first officially approved by Yunnan Province, the China–Laos Mohan-Boten Economic Cooperative Zone is a frontier window for Yunnan Province to build an economic center facing South Asia and Southeast Asia. In recent years, their bilateral economic and trade cooperation has been steadily growing. The two sides have seized opportunities in areas such as investment promotion, resource allocation, and mechanized innovation and achieved beneficial results.

In 2022, the import and export volume of bilateral goods between China and Laos was US$504.81878 billion, an increase of US$107.19924 billion compared with the same period in 2021, and an annual increase of 27.2%. The operation of the China–Laos Railway and the implementation of the RCEP Agreement have provided a stronger engine for bilateral economic development. On this occasion, Yunnan Province responded actively and issued policies and measures, such as the Three-Year Action Plan for Implementing the Important Speech of President Xi Jinping for Developing and Constructing the China–Laos Railway and the Yunnan Province Action Plan for Accelerating the Connection with the RCEP. The international freight trains on the China–Laos Railway have provided the "Lancang-Mekong Express" products, and new forms of trade, such as cross-border e-commerce, are riding the momentum.

In 2021, the Commodity Exhibition and Investment and Trade Fair for South and Southeast Asian Countries was held. At the First China–Laos Mohan-Boten Economic Cooperative Zone for Joint Investment Promotion Conference, entitled "New Opportunities, New Measures, and New Development," the Management Committee launched 17 investment projects with a total investment of more than RMB 23 billion. In the prevention and control of COVID-19, the ports adhere to the management principles of the "separation of people and goods, segmented transportation, and closed management," and strictly implement measures such as checking and disinfecting every truck to minimize the risk of importing COVID-19 at the ports, which made important contributions to the epidemic prevention and control of Yunnan, and even the whole country. Affinity between the peoples leads to state-to-state friendship and also leads to mutual understanding. Connected by mountains and rivers, China and Laos have always shared the same heart, friendship, and sincerity. Today, with a frequent amount of good news, the cooperative zone will embrace greater and broader development opportunities in multiple fields and levels, such as deeper cross-border industrial cooperation, bilateral economic trade, border development, and globalization.

In May 2022, Kunming officially took over the responsibility for Mohan Town of Xishuangbanna, marking the important occasion that Kunming has become the only provincial capital city with a "borderline" in China. It is an important initiative that gives full play to the advantages of the four districts (Kunming District, Economic Development Zone, Comprehensive Bonded Zone, and Mohan-Boten Economic Cooperative Zone). The adjustment of this pattern is a pioneering exploration to break down the institutional mechanism and policy barriers and is also the first of its kind in China.

Mohan Port

In 2023, 119 key projects with a total investment of RMB 91.925 billion are planned in the China–Laos Mohan-Boten Cooperation Zone. The same year, the total volume of import and export of goods at the Mohan Port amounted to around 8.025 million tonnes, an increase of 41.61%, and the total value of import and export goods was about RMB 47.27 billion, an increase of 9.07% year-on-year, and the number of people entering and exiting the country reached 1.45 million, an increase of 374.1%.

China-Myanmar Ruili-Muse Cross-Border Economic Cooperative Zone

The cooperative zone is located in Ruili City, Dehong Dai, and Jingpo autonomous prefecture of Yunnan Province, adjacent to the China-Myanmar border. It was originally planned to cover an area of 64 square kilometers (among which, the seine zone covers an area of 12.94 square kilometers). The cooperative zone includes Jiegao, Nongdao, Mangling, Wanding and importing and exporting processing zones. Since the Chinese side put forward the idea in 2007, fruitful achievements have been made with unremitting efforts. In 2017, China and Myanmar officially signed the Memorandum of Understanding between the Ministry of Commerce of China and the Ministry of Commerce of Myanmar on the Construction of the China-Myanmar Border Economic Cooperative Zone, which marked substantial progress that has been made in the bilateral economic cooperative zone. In October 2012, Ruili and Mushi signed a sister-city relationship agreement and held the China-Myanmar Border Trade Fair and the China-Myanmar Carnival for several years.

As the largest land port in Myanmar, Muse Port plays two important roles in Myanmar, namely the important trade port, and its also in the special economic zone for globalization. The regional financing platform has accelerated bilateral financing efforts, and the e-commerce platform operated by the Jiegao Trade and Promotion E-commerce Company in Myanmar, offers an online payment system using kyat. At the same time, the Ruili Cross-Border Investment Co., Ltd. is engaged in infrastructure investment in the China-Myanmar Ruili-Mujie joint border Zone. Relying on eMyan, an export-oriented cross-border e-commerce sales platform, China has made significant progress in cross-border commerce and trade, supplying the largest e-commerce platform in Myanmar in 2019.

In 1956, Premier Zhou Enlai and Prime Minister Ba swe of Myanmar crossed the Wanding Bridge on foot. Wanding is a major station on China's an-

Ruili Port

Wanding Port

cient Southern Silk Road, with a long history of trade. As far back as the Han Dynasty (202 BC-AD 220), it had become an important distribution center for merchants and prospered until the Qing Dynasty. Wanding Town is separated from Myanmar by a river with a long stream that nourishes both banks. Its borderline is about 28 kilometers, forming a unique cultural landscape of "one city and two countries" with Jiugu City, Myanmar. For a long time, people on the border of China and Myanmar have been trading and marrying each other and have been living in the same ethnic group across the border, thus truly reflecting the nature of friendship while singing songs and drinking water together, into their daily lives. The two peoples are brothers and their blood is thicker than water. It is common for Myanmar people to come to Wanding to study or for medical treatment. Moreover, in Wanding, the architectural style is also unique. A number of architectural styles are evident including a mixture of Nanyang styles, ethnic styles, and Thai and Burmese styles form the unique beauty of the local scenery. The beauty of nature and the peaceful landscape, the beauty of scattered and interwoven space structures, the beauty of having a colorful history and humanity, and the beauty of a fresh and refined pastoral landscape are organically integrated, which not only has the graceful and artistic style of Jiangnan (the southern part of China), but it also has the enthusiasm and vitality of Dali.

Pursuit of Sustainable Development

Sustainable Economic Development

Economic and sustainable development is one of the three pillars of LMC. The 2030 Agenda for Sustainable Development is an important topic in global and regional governance. In ancient China, there was a consistent developmental concept of "saving lands for future generations." Its core connotation has something in common with sustainable development. The concept of the green economy is becoming an important way for people to think about future economic development. Green economic development in the Lancang-Mekong region has closely followed the theme of the times. It actively cooperated with ASEAN, adopting the global concept of green development and the principle of combining local conditions, so that the concept of sustainable development has gradually spread to all Lancang-Mekong countries.

In 2019, the 34th ASEAN Summit adopted the Bangkok Declaration on combating marine waste, which became the first ASEAN agreement on managing marine waste. In 2019, the Climate Bond Initiative issued the ASEAN Green Finance Instrument Guide, providing a guidance framework for the development of green finance in the ASEAN region. Among the Lancang-Mekong countries, the Thailand Board of Investment revised the national strategic investment promotion plan to ensure that it is consistent with the latest national and global trends. The Bio-Cycling-Green Economy Model economic model created by the plan has become a benchmark for green economic development in the region.

The "Green Spring Breeze" Brought about by the Biodiversity Conference

The COP15 was held in Kunming, Yunnan Province in 2021. Yunnan Province and the Mekong countries have conducted closer cooperation in biodiversity conservation, climate change and low-carbon development. In the future, the establishment of effective and fully functional Lancang-Mekong low-carbon industrial parks will become a banner of green economic development in the Lancang-Mekong region. However, the governments of the Lancang-Mekong countries still face realistic challenges of how to achieve fair and effective transitions, including

UNITED NATIONS
BIODIVERSITY CONFERENCE
(COP15) Kunming, China 2021

2020 UN BIODIVERSITY CONFERENCE
C O P 1 5 - C P / M O P 1 0 - N P / M O P 4
Ecological Civilization-Building a Shared Future for All Life on Earth
KUNMING CHINA

Convention on
Biological Diversity

The logo of COP15 Conference

how to adjust the economic and energy structure, and how to achieve the coordinated improvement of environmental quality in the process of transition.

The Cooperative Philosophy of "Breathing Together and Sharing the Same Destiny"

The LMC reflects the cooperative philosophy of a community with a shared future, which means breathing together and sharing the same destiny. At the Sixth LMC Foreign Ministers' Meeting held in Chongqing on June 8, 2021, all parties agreed that strengthening the management of water resources along the Lancang-Mekong River and closer cooperation among the riparian countries, were crucial to promoting sustainable regional economic and social development. They also appreciated the positive progress that has been made in the Lancang-Mekong ecological and environmental cooperation, such as the achievements in strengthening cooperation and sharing experiences regarding clean and renewable energy, jointly promoting a green and low-carbon transformation, and boosting their ability to deal with climate change.

The Green Lancang-Mekong Initiative That Has Been Put into Practice

The Green Lancang-Mekong Initiative: Lancang-Mekong Roundtable Dialogue on Green, Low-Carbon, and Sustainable Infrastructure was held in Beijing in April 2022, and the conference discussed important issues related to the sustainable development of the Lancang-Mekong economy, covering many areas of production. For example, in the fields of agriculture and forestry, shrubs and herbaceous cash crops can be combined with rubber plantations and poultry raising in forests, to improve the traditional single rubber plantation model and solve the contradiction between ecological problems caused by the planting of rubber and the improvement of the community's livelihood.

The environmental rubber plantations in Mengla Longlin, Jingtai, and the Naban River watershed are demonstration projects for the construction of environment-friendly ecological rubber plantations in Yunnan Province. The parks have changed their planting structures, introducing tea, coffee, cocoa, and medicinal crops, and investing in the research of carbon sequestration in rubber forests to maximize their value. In addition to Yunnan, the Jiangnan Manufacturing Comprehensive Development Zone in Guigang, Guangxi, has also achieved full coverage of heating through a biomass cogeneration project that uses agricultural

The monument of the earliest rubber plantation in Xishuangbanna

and forestry waste as fuel. By replacing coal with agricultural and forestry biomass energy, it not only reduces carbon emissions, but also creates new opportunities for becoming prosperous through the establishment of green employment and has achieved an outstanding demonstration effect and become a role model.

Coffee is an important value-based crop in Yunnan. In recent years, while improving product quality and optimizing the supply chain, Yunnan Province has also given consideration to the improvement of environmental protection awareness of coffee farmers. For example, the ECOM group has implemented over 300 sustainable development projects globally, managing 600,000 farmers directly involved in planting. In Yunnan, the mixed agroforestry coffee planting system has become a new highlight in coffee cultivation. In the future, new breakthroughs of sustainable development models in coffee may be made in this province and sharing new planting experiences will also benefit countries in the entire Lancang-Mekong River Basin.

The eight main regions in Yunnan for coffee production

Sustainable Development Extends Its Roots Deeper and Wider

Sustainable development has always been an important area of pragmatic cooperation between China and countries along the Mekong River. Therefore, all parties work together to lead the sustainable development in the region, making important contributions to the implementation of the 2030 Agenda for Sustainable Development, which stems from the United Nations. China and ASEAN officially announced the establishment of a comprehensive strategic partnership for peace, security, prosperity, and sustainable development, setting a new milestone in the history of bilateral relations in November 2021. The year 2022 is the first year of the China-ASEAN comprehensive strategic partnership and the second year of the China-ASEAN sustainable development cooperation, which continues to broaden and become more concrete between the two sides in areas such as being green, achieving low-carbon emissions, clean energy, climate change, and ecological protection. In November 2022, China and ASEAN issued a China-ASEAN Joint Statement on Strengthening Common and Sustainable Development, stating that China and ASEAN will jointly promote a healthy environment for global and regional development, maintain regional peace, stability, and security, share development opportunities, and promote the realization of sustainable development goals globally and regionally.

To Sow in Spring and Harvest in Autumn, We Weather the Weal and Woe Together

A seed planted in spring will yield a full harvest in autumn. In the areas of agriculture and poverty reduction, the people of the six countries have jointly planted the seeds of agricultural development and poverty alleviation. Now, the abundant harvest has borne fruit and the people are enjoying the joy of a bountiful harvest. As the saying goes, "the fragrance of plum blossoms comes from the bitter cold," in spite of the negative impact of COVID-19 pandemic on economic growth, the cooperation between agriculture and poverty reduction has gone through tests and will eventually continue with an unwavering determination and embrace challenges with a smile, like a blossoming plum tree, in the wind and snow.

Meticulous Farming Yields Shining Rice

The Fourth LMC Leaders' Meeting was held on December 25, 2003, in which the leaders of the six countries agreed to support the green and sustainable development of agriculture and enhance the competitiveness of agricultural products. The Sixth Lancang-Mekong Business Forum was held in Beijing on January 10, 2024, with the theme of "Promoting Agribusiness and Investment in Processed Food Sector," aiming to promote exchanges and cooperation among agricultural enterprises of the six countries and build a platform to share experiences.

As one of the five priorities of the LMC, since the launch of the LMC agricultural cooperation mechanism, the six countries have made joint efforts to continuously improve cooperative planning and practical cooperation. With the support of the LMC Special Fund, a series of agricultural projects benefiting the people's livelihoods have been implemented, which have played a positive role in improving the level of regional agricultural technology, promoting agricultural mutual investment and trade, increasing farmers' income, and serving the construction of the economic development belt in the Lancang-Mekong Basin.

Agricultural Cooperation Takes Root in the Fertile LMC Soil

Established in 2017, the LMC Agriculture Joint Working Group is an institutional platform for Lancang-Mekong agricultural cooperation, whose main objectives are improving the coordinated development of agriculture in the sub-regions, ensuring food (nutrition) security and safety, promoting cooperation in agricultural investment and trade, and facilitating agricultural exchanges and sustainable development.

In January 2019, the Ministry of Agriculture and Rural Affairs of China officially established the Lancang-Mekong Agricultural Cooperation Center, which is the third center under the LMC mechanism and will continue to provide support and services for agricultural cooperation.

To strengthen communication, the LMC Village Chiefs Forum has established a platform for policy communication, experience exchanges, and economic and trade-related cooperation in agriculture and rural areas in the Lancang-Mekong region. In order to improve the level of agricultural development, exchanges, and cooperation in agricultural science and technology have been continuously enhanced, and multi-aspect cooperative platforms have been founded for technology promotion, information exchange, prevention and control of animal and plant diseases, and the quality and safety of agricultural products.

The achievements of the Lancang-Mekong agricultural cooperation mechanism reflect real needs that need to be met in agricultural cooperation, which can truly take root in the land and show the farmers' needs.

Just like a tree with deep and extensive roots, the Lancang-Mekong agricultural cooperation is rooted in the real needs of the people, which is why the agricultural cooperation mechanism has been continuously consolidated.

Technical Exchanges Cultivate Agricultural Projects

The vitality of a tree is reflected in its branches, leaves, and flowers, while dense branches and leaves which draw nutrients from the roots and then transport them to the whole tree, represent various technical exchange projects.

The China–Laos Cooperation Crop Variety Test Station was established in Vientiane, Laos, in 2013.

China conducted workshops on improved rice production technology with four countries in the Lancang-Mekong River including Cambodia, Myanmar, Laos, and Vietnam, in 2018.

The nine-day 2021 online training course for Vietnamese agricultural management and technical personnel was successfully completed on September 7, 2021.

The online Training Workshop on Lancang-Mekong Agro Products Quality and Safety Inspection and Testing was successfully held on September 13, 2021.

The opening ceremony of the agricultural technology training project in Siem Reap, Cambodia, was held in Kunming, Yunnan Province, on October 25, 2021.

The Training Course on Improved Varieties Breeding of Tropical Crops for Myanmar was launched online, and 22 students from Myanmar participated in the 21-day course on November 16, 2021.

The online training course on the processing and preservation of agricultural products in Myanmar was launched on May 18, 2022.

On the "big tree" of agricultural cooperation, the branches of technical exchanges such as personnel training, good seed cultivation, and quality testing, have spread along the Lancang-Mekong River. Interwoven and interconnected to each other, they bring abundant vitality and greenery to the earth.

If technical exchanges are compared to branches and leaves, then special agricultural projects are blooming flowers clustered thickly on the branches, allowing everyone who nurtured them to smell their fragrance.

Like blooming flowers, numerous agricultural projects are being provided for by the Lancang-Mekong Special Fund.

A total of RMB 230 million from the fund has been provided to support agricultural projects until April 23, 2021.

The agricultural departments of the six countries have implemented a series of projects benefiting the people's livelihoods with the support of the Lancang-Mekong Special Fund. The Ministry of Agriculture and Rural Affairs of China has carried out nearly 30 projects, covering multiple areas such as rice, natural rubber, and fisheries, with some key provinces such as Guangxi and Yunnan provinces in China, as well as a group of scientific research institutions and universities that possess technological advantages, as participants. These projects involve multiple stages, such as production, processing, etc., and the executive functions include the provisions of guidance, exchanges and training, and park construction.

The flowers bloom in their own unique ways, and the agricultural projects that stem from the LMC have their own characteristics.

In the project for establishing and improving the quality assurance system of processing small and medium-scale fishery products in Myanmar, water purification equipment has been installed to solve water safety problems for traditional fishery products.

The project for increasing coffee production has trained over 11,000 Myanmar coffee farmers, helping to improve its quality, and double the output of coffee in Myanmar.

The project for the production of high-yielding rice varieties has developed better rice varieties that are resistant to lodging and against waterlogging, with shorter growth cycles that result in improved qualities and production.

The project for establishing a rapid clonal propagation nursey for mangoes, grapefruits, jackfruits and guavas has founded a horticultural demonstration farm, which will conduct technical exchanges and training with the local community to promote the development of the fruit industry.

The project of the Demonstration of Integration of Natural Rubber Cultivation and Processing Technology Lancang-Mekong Countries has enabled China to export its self-cultivated tissue-cultured seedlings of rubber trees to Cambodia, thereby helping to promote the sustainable development of the rubber industry in Cambodia.

The investigation into the Cambodian pepper market has improved the production technology of pepper in Cambodia and opened a new chapter for cooperation in the pepper industry between China and Cambodia.

The project for promoting economic development through the further processing of fruit in the Lancang-Mekong region has helped these countries extend their fruit industrial chains and increase added-values.

The project to promote agricultural product values and production capacity exchanges in the Lancang-Mekong countries through the use of innovative technologies has helped the food processing industry reduce its environmental impact and satisfy consumers' tastes and preferences.

In addition, the fund has also supported projects such as vegetable and fruit cultivation, rubber planting, and silkworm breeding, helping local people to increase their production and income.

The trees are shady and the fragrance of flowers is overwhelming, making summer the perfect time for agricultural cooperation.

Bountiful Harvest of Industrial and Trade Cooperation Shared with Joy

The fragrance of melon and fruit is people's first impression of countries in the Lancang-Mekong region and it is also a major feature of the import and export in agricultural products between China and these countries. In 2022, China's imports of fruits from Mekong countries amounted to RMB 54.141 billion and exports reached RMB 13.14 billion.

Trains full of fruit and vegetables shuttle back-and-forth between the countries in the Mekong River region. They carry bananas, watermelons, passion fruits, citrus fruits from Laos, bananas, mangoes, and longans from Cambodia, mangoes, durians, longans, lychees, and mangosteens from Thailand, and pineapples, mangoes, pitayas, rambutans, watermelons, bananas, longans, lychees, and mangosteens from Vietnam, delivering them to various parts of China and also bring apples, pears, citrus fruits, grapes, and dates from China to the tables of people who live in the Mekong River region.

The rice is golden, and the fruit and vegetables are fragrant. Nowadays, we can taste delicious food from thousands of miles away without having to travel long distances. Longans from Thailand are crystally clear and transparent, mangosteens from Vietnam are sour and sweet, citrus fruits from Laos are refreshing and juicy, and bananas from Cambodia are soft and delicious ... Not only are there more and more types of fruit on the market, but the price is also gradually decreasing. The agricultural cooperation in the Mekong River region has achieved "fruit freedom"—buying fruit without taking the price into consideration, allowing the six countries to share the joy of this harvest.

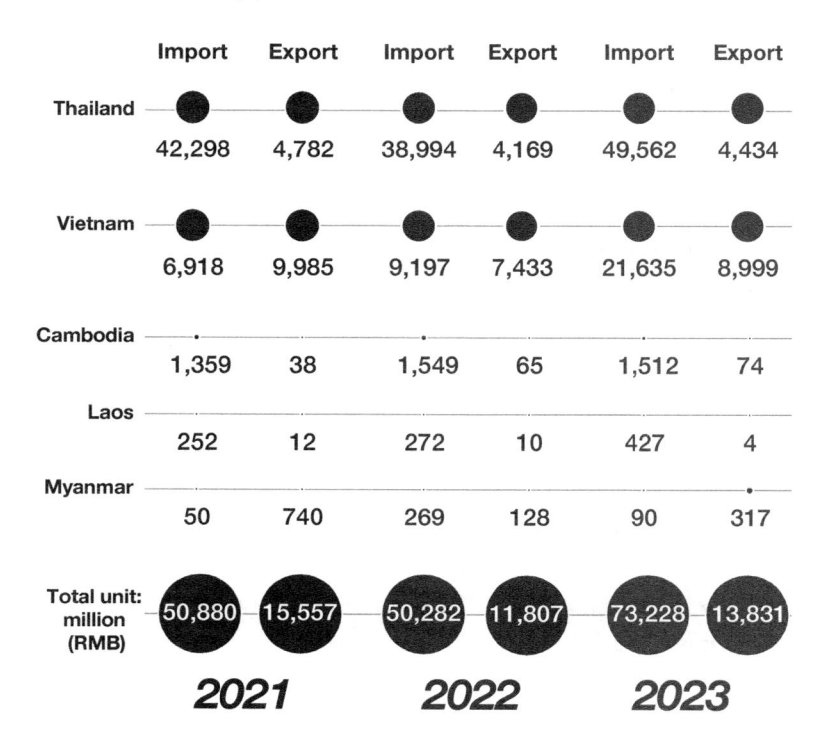

	Import	Export	Import	Export	Import	Export
Thailand	42,298	4,782	38,994	4,169	49,562	4,434
Vietnam	6,918	9,985	9,197	7,433	21,635	8,999
Cambodia	1,359	38	1,549	65	1,512	74
Laos	252	12	272	10	427	4
Myanmar	50	740	269	128	90	317
Total unit: million (RMB)	50,880	15,557	50,282	11,807	73,228	13,831
	2021		**2022**		**2023**	

The export and import of edible fruits, nuts, sweet melons, and citrus fruits between China and the five countries along the Mekong River

The Life of a Seed

I am an ordinary rice seed, but also an extraordinary hybrid rice seed. I come from China, but the place where I really took root and sprouted is Myanmar.

As a hybrid grain of rice, my greatest advantage is high yield. On one *mu* of land, about 666 square meters, I can produce up to 550 kilograms, twice the yield of Myanmar's rice seeds. In addition, each member of my family also has its own unique edge, such as resistance to lodging, rice blast disease, and brown planthoppers.

When we grow in the fields, people often come to check on our growth. The experimenters implement different methods of irrigation and apply different types of fertilizers to test which one can allow us to grow better.

Under their careful care, the rice fields are filled with golden rice ready to be harvested. People smile as they harvest in the fields, and we finally board the train back to our hometown, China.

In our hometown, we are eventually processed in a rice processing factory where we become rice products such as rice noodles and rice vermicelli, that will be sent to different destinations.

A wide river that has rolling waves, the fragrance of rice flowers on both banks is carried by the wind. Traveling between the two hometowns of birth and growth, I will bring happy smiles to the people there.

Reduce Poverty to Brighten Thousands of Households

When the Chinese Premier attended the ASEAN Plus Three (Japan-China-Republic of Korea) Summit on November 13, 2014, he stated that narrowing the gap, reducing poverty, and improving people's livelihoods are the top priorities for Asian countries. China proposed the East Asian Cooperation Initiative on Poverty Reduction and pledged to provide RMB 100 million to carry out the plan for rural poverty alleviation and to establish a demonstration project for poverty reduction cooperation in East Asia. In November 2020, the Chinese Premier attended the 23rd APT Summit and expressed China's willingness to implement the second phase of the East Asian Cooperation Initiative on Poverty Reduction to achieve regional coordinated development.

The Past and Present after the Initiative

The China-East Asia Poverty Reduction Demonstration Cooperation Technical Assistance Project has selected Laos, Cambodia, and Myanmar as its pilot countries, and it will take three years to set up two project sites in each country, a total of six villages for implementation.

The project involves four aspects, including infrastructure construction, improvement of public service facilities and the people's livelihood, technical assistance, and capacity development.

In terms of infrastructure, the project has greatly improved living conditions and the water supply in the selected villages. Forty-two houses have been rebuilt and 148 houses have been renovated and the construction of drinking water projects has met the needs of safe drinking water for more than 800 households in Cambodia; the project for household water supply has covered 581 villagers in Laos; and 1,282 farmers have now gained access to clean drinking water in the two targeted villages in Myanmar.

In terms of public service facilities, several activity centers, schools, and medical clinics have been built. In Cambodia, a newly built community activity center with a construction area of 400 square meters has become a comprehensive one-stop public service platform for local villages. In Laos, facilities such as village activity centers, health clinics, and student dormitories have been constructed. In

Myanmar, facilities such as classrooms, libraries, and sports fields have been built, greatly improving the local educational conditions.

In terms of improving people's livelihood, relying on local resources is the first choice. In Cambodia, demonstration activities for traditional planting methods have been carried out, and two detergent processing plants have been built to help villagers find local employment. At the same time, Chinese chef training has been implemented to encourage villagers to work outside the village. Two demonstration villages in Laos have also carried out activities related to animal husbandry and tourism and have elected corresponding committees and groups to manage projects for poverty alleviation. In Myanmar, activities regarding crop improvement have been executed to continuously improve the quality and efficiency of traditional industries.

In terms of the provision of technical assistance and capacity development, two-way communication has achieved the effect of 1 + 1 > 2. In the villages that are implementing the project in Cambodia, one round of management training, four rounds of skills training, and two rounds of practical technology training have been carried out, and two training sessions have been organized within China. In Laos, various management and technical training activities have been conducted eight times, and two training sessions have been held in China, while in Myanmar, the figure was nine rounds of field training and one training session in China.

Four thousand people have had access to tap water, 82 households have had access to electricity, 71 households have had their houses rebuilt, 190 households

Pilot villages for the Eastern China Asian Poverty Reduction Demonstration Cooperative Technical Assistance Project

have had their houses renovated, 132 households have had new toilets installed, 500 households are using firewood-saving stoves, 200 households are implementing courtyard economy, 80 households are growing millet peppers, 28 households are engaging in the cultivation of high-temperature mushrooms, 40 households have become model cattle breeders, and 2 detergent processing factories have been built ... The data from the poverty reduction demonstration villages confirms China's contributions to poverty reduction in Cambodia.

People used to say, "Our health has been affected because of water problems," but now they say, "We now have access to safe drinking water and no longer have to worry about water quality issues."

Students used to say, "Going to the toilet is inconvenient; there is a lot of garbage behind the school," but the discourse has now become, "The school now has a library, and we can come and read books anytime, making it convenient for us to acquire knowledge."

People used to say, "Back then, both inside and outside the village were dirt roads. During the rainy season, cars got stuck, and during the dry season, we ate dust," but now they say, "Now, driving and cycling are smooth and comfortable."

The contrast in the discourse highlights the enormous changes that have taken place since the initiative was proposed. The once desolate and underdeveloped villages have become a place where people can live and work in peace and contentment, and the driving force behind this transformation is the East Asian Cooperation Initiative on Poverty Reduction.

An Open Land of the Peach Blossom in 21st Century

"The land is spacious and flat, the houses are neat and well-ordered, and there are fertile fields, beautiful ponds, and groves of mulberry and bamboo. Paths and roads intersect the village, and the crowing of roosters and the barking of dogs could be heard. Men and women go about their farming and weaving dressed in foreign clothes. The old and the young all seem content and happy."

This is the utopia described in "Peach Blossom Spring" and also in Xienglom Village in Luang Prabang, Laos, with the implementation of the poverty reduction project. Its only difference from "Peach Blossom Spring" is that this is an open-style utopian society in the 21st century.

In the past, when the sun set, the whole village became pitch black. As we enter the 21st century, lights illuminate every household in Xienglom Village, lighting up the once-dark night.

Working at sunrise and resting at sunset used to be a traditional practice that followed the natural rhythm of day and night, but also a result of limited options that existed in the past. Nowadays, with the availability of electricity, people can entertain themselves by watching television and conversing with family members under the warm and cozy light after a day's work. Laughter and joy now fill the previously silent and dark night.

From the narrow and difficult beginnings to the sudden spaciousness, the road has not only opened the door for people to the outside world, but it has also promoted the development of industries along the way.

Sima, a villager in Xienglom Village, is 70 years old this year. In her eyes, the cooperative project for poverty reduction between China and Laos has brought tangible changes to her life.

Newly constructed roads in Laos

She said: "There were no streetlights before, and it was pitch black at night. Now, when night falls, villagers gather under the streetlights to chat, and children run around, making it much livelier."

In addition to building roads, the installation of solar streetlights locally has solved the transportation difficulties for over 2,800 villagers in two villages, provided a convenient channel for the development of the vegetable industry and folk tourism in the village, and improved the living standards of the villagers.

Now, in Xienglom Village, the roads are neat and tidy, and the houses are clean. Children study in the newly built school and run in the playground while the villagers are all skilled and hardworking. The village, with its red roofs and white-walled houses, contrasts beautifully with the green hills and clear waters surrounding it, making it a veritable paradise on earth.

The Road to Prosperity with Distinctive Characteristics

On the numerous roads leading to prosperity, establishing one's own distinct characteristics is the key. In this regard, the Lancang-Mekong countries have the most say.

» *Surprise the World with a Brilliant Feat*

Raising chickens is a "traditional industry" in Xienglom Village, but it used to be scattered among the households, with each household raising only a few to a dozen chickens. The demonstration project for poverty reduction discovered the hidden advantages of the chicken-raising industry, which brought economies of scale to the villagers.

Due to the impact of the COVID-19 pandemic, as well as the shortage of chicks, rising prices, and the unsuitability of Egyptian chickens to the temperature and climate in northern Laos, coupled with the farmers' inadequate insulation measures, the initial attempt to raise chickens failed with many young chicks dying.

However, the project team did not become discouraged; rather, they clarified their responsibilities, investigated the reasons, and bore the losses of the first attempt, accumulating experience in purchasing chicks for the second attempt.

Before the second purchase, they learned lessons, conducted training in advance, and purchased local chickens from Laos to prioritize stability.

These chicken chicks grew well, and after about four months of raising, each chicken grew to about 1.5 kilograms in size and sold for 50,000 to 60,000 kip (about RMB 40). They were all sold out, and each household received an average of RMB 5,000 in net income. The project was a success. Having tasted the benefits of chicken-raising, the team members have organized the third batch of chick purchases and are full of confidence in continuing to develop the chicken-raising industry.

» *Weaving a Happy Future*

In Laos, women commonly wear traditional ethnic costumes, and as long as the fabrics are innovative in design and reliable in quality, there will be no concerns for sales.

Ban Xor Village has had a tradition of weaving since ancient times and has accumulated rich experience over the years. However, due to decentralized production, small-scale, limited funding, and limited product varieties, their weaving is at a competitive disadvantage in the market.

Since 2018, with the help of the coordination office for China–Laos joint projects, Ban Xor Village has independently decided to make weaving one of the main development projects in the village. The weaving group purchased weaving equipment, which was collectively owned by the village, so they paid for its usage and purchased the needed production materials with available project funds.

In August 2020, the weaving exhibition hall, which was constructed with assistance from China, in Ban Xor Village, was completed. Villagers brought their own woven products for an exhibition, which attracted many people to come and purchase.

Villager Ni Campafonsha, nearly 50 years old, joined a weaving group composed of more than 20 households. As a part-time job, she can increase her income by about RMB 4,000 a year from weaving. The poverty reduction team plans to promote these products by establishing an online sales network, creating a trademark, and building a model that combines unified marketing and the members' independent marketing. It is estimated that the average annual net income of each household is expected to reach RMB 8,720.

» *Mushrooms with Magic*

Mushroom cultivation in Svay Ampear Commune, Mok Kampoul District, Kandal Province, Cambodia, has led the village on a path of poverty alleviation and prosperity.

The local climate is extremely suitable for growing mushrooms at high temperatures. The expert team built mushroom sheds for farmers, purchased materials such as mushroom seeds and bags, and invited professional technicians to provide guidance on-site.

Zhu Jin was one of the first farmers to grow mushrooms. "Our family started growing mushrooms in April this year, and we harvested a total of more than 1,200 kilograms of mushrooms in four months." He said, smiling from ear to ear, "I am very grateful to the Chinese experts. I have also learned how to make mushroom spawns and bags."

» *Being Famous Around the World*

There is a traditional craft of making brass gongs in Ban Sai Mun, Ubon Ratchathani, in northeastern Thailand. With support from the government, the local traditional handicraft gongs are not only sold in Thailand, but also exported overseas.

Chaiwa, a senior artist who made gongs, said that he earned tens of thousands of Thai baht every month.

Give a Man a Fish and You Feed Him for a Day; Teach a Man to Fish and You Feed Him for a Lifetime

In 2020, China has made great progress in its poverty alleviation efforts and Chinese have waved goodbye to absolute poverty, This achievement has not only significantly contributed to the global fight against poverty, but also allowed the Mekong countries to recognize China's lessons in terms of poverty eradication and widely learn from Chinese experience.

Nguyen Vuillay (not sure about the spelling of the name), the then Laotian Director of the Confucius Institute at the National University of Laos, commented, "China's achievements in fighting poverty are world-renowned and have provided effective strategies for overcoming poverty. Laos and other countries may learn from China."

Uk Rabun, Minister of Rural Development of Cambodia, pointed out, "China's successful development experience has inspired us to implement some important projects in Cambodia, including the China-aided Rural Road Project and the China-aided Rural Water Supply Project. The poverty reduction cooperation under the LMC has provided a strong impetus for Cambodia's rural economy."

Vice Minister of Commerce of Thailand, Sansern Samalapa, said, "I think the Chinese government has carried out poverty alleviation policies very precisely and efficiently. There are several points that are really worth learning, such as implementing targeted poverty alleviation measures based on the specific conditions of different groups and regions, building a moderately prosperous society in all aspects, and making sure no one has been left behind on the road to common prosperity, vigorously developing education and health care in poverty-stricken areas, using tax leverage to regulate the distribution of social wealth and narrow the gap between the rich and the poor, and developing an efficient assessment system for poverty alleviation achievements."

China's experience in fighting poverty has taken root in the Mekong River Basin with two key examples being paired assistance model and targeted poverty alleviation measures.

The paired assistance model has been applied in Khon Kaen, Thailand.

Khon Kaen officials have traveled to China specifically to study poverty alleviation experiences. After returning to Thailand, they developed paired assistance poverty alleviation project tailored to local conditions, which help create specific poverty alleviation plans for impoverished families. This practice of sending poverty alleviation officials to rural areas to offer paired assistance was unprecedented in Thailand.

Thanakorn, an official from the Agriculture Bureau of Bamnet Narong county in Khon Kaen Province, who was undertaking poverty alleviation work in Nonnokham village, said that Khon Kaen Province followed China's practice of creating files for impoverished families, collecting data on household population, occupations, income, vocational skill level of the main laborers, and the causes of poverty for each family. Based on these surveys, poverty alleviation officials would study how to provide targeted assistance to families who are in need.

"In the process of poverty alleviation, we require poverty alleviation officials to share the hardships with the impoverished families, and whenever they go to the villages, they should listen to the villagers, find the problems and work out solutions." Khon Kaen Governor Somsak said, "These are all experiences we learned from China."

Bon Song, a Nonnokham villager in his forties, told reporters that under the guidance of poverty alleviation officials, his family has raised chickens, fish, and vegetables. Part of the produce was daily food supplies for the family, and the rest were sold, leading to a continous increase in the household income.

Somkid, the son of the poor Santi family in Nongnokham village, participated in vocational training provided by the government for villagers. After Somkid had mastered motorcycle repair techniques, the poverty alleviation officials recommended him to work in a repair store in town. With a stable income, the family's living condition gradually improved.

"Thanks to the paired assistance from the poverty alleviation project, we have acquired skills to make a living," said Bon Song, who used to worry about every meal and now is able to save nearly 2,000 baht a month.

In addition, drawing lessons from China's precise approach to poverty alleviation, Thailand has built a poverty reduction platform to collect information from poor regions and identify impoverished households.

The Thai Deputy Prime Minister Wissanu said, "We need to learn from China's technological approach to poverty alleviation, work with technological and digital business enterprises to precisely identify poor families, and vigorously develop agriculture and infrastructure in rural areas. As for personnel arrangements, inspired by the Chinese model of sending grassroots officials to impoverished areas, we are cooperating with universities nationwide to work out poverty reduction strategies, assigning one university to support several poverty locations and sending college students to those areas for help."

Working Together and Offering Mutual Support

The Expert Team Rose to the Challenge

The outbreak of COVID-19 has been a heavy blow to the world. Yet China and the five Mekong countries stood by and supported each other, effectively controlled the spread of the pandemic in the region, and created a model of inter-regional cooperation in fighting the coronavirus. To help the Mekong countries improve their epidemic prevention and governance capacity, China has organized technical exchanges by holding teleconferences and expert webinars and provided a large number of medical supplies such as masks, protective suits, and nucleic acid test kits to help the Mekong countries overcome difficulties.

The year 2021 undoubtedly witnessed the most severe pandemic in Southeast Asia. Fearlessly, the Chinese medical expert team forged ahead toward the harsh environment of the raging virus to share their experiences of pandemic prevention and control with Laos, which was struck hard by COVID-19. China stood by Laos to overcome the severest period of the pandemic. Time was life, of which the medical expert team sent by Chinese government were very clear. During the two weeks in Laos, the team planned its route scientifically to learn as much as possible about the pandemic situation in Laos to maximize the effectiveness of their assistance.

On May 4, 2021, right after getting off the plane, the expert team inspected a number of quarantine hotels in the Laotian capital of Vientiane, where they guided the management process and disinfection norms.

On the 5th and 6th, to understand the actual conditions in the hospitals and visit the patients, the expert team visited several designated hospitals for COVID-19 patients that were under great pressure.

On May 7, the expert team visited several new coronavirus sampling sites to examine the sampling process, information collection, criteria for determining close contacts and the disinfection measures.

From May 9 to May 14, the expert team went to Luang Prabang, Bokeo, Oudomxay, and Luang Namtha provinces in northern Laos, where the pandemic was serious. They investigated the local epidemic prevention and control measures and offered guidance to the working team on site.

On May 18, the Ministry of Health of Laos held a review meeting with the expert team and awarded honorary certificates to the team members successively. In just one fortnight, the expert team visited various places in Laos and were like sparks warming the cold winter night.

In front of the expert team sat the neighboring country, who were in dire straits, and behind them were their beloved families and friends who were far away. Yet fearlessly they rose to the challenge, passing the flames of hope, which grew increasingly higher and brighter, from hand to hand in fighting against the epidemic.

Vaccines Aid the Mekong Countries During Life-and-Death Moments

Vaccination is an important measure to control the coronavirus pandemic. Since the outbreak, China has insisted on donating vaccines to the Mekong countries even when faced with capacity constraints and huge demand at home. At the Third LMC Leaders' Meeting held on August 24, 2020, the Chinese Premier clearly announced that "Chinese coronavirus vaccines will be provided to the Mekong countries on a priority basis as soon as China finishes the vaccine development process and put them into use." China has had very close interactions with the five Mekong countries in vaccine production and procurement, which has built a security shield for the region.

On February 8, 2022, Xiong Bo, the Chinese Ambassador to Vietnam, said that strengthening joint efforts against COVID-19 is a priority area of current China-Vietnam cooperation, and China has provided a total of 52 million doses of vaccines to Vietnam, which has made positive contributions to Vietnam's coordinated epidemic prevention and control and social, economic development.

As of March 30, 2022, China has provided 42 million doses of COVID-19 vaccines to Cambodia and become the most important and reliable supplier of vaccines to the country.

As of June 30, 2022, China has provided 51 million doses of vaccines to Myanmar and facilitated the local filling.

The "Spring Sprout" campaign is a COVID-19 vaccination program for overseas Chinese during the outbreak of the pandemic. To carry out this campaign, not only does it require proactive action from China, but also full cooperation from the host countries. Since the day when Wang Yi, the State Councilor and Foreign Minister of China, announced the launch of the "Spring Sprout" campaign in March 2021, it has gradually taken root in the Mekong River Basin based on mutual understanding and support.

In addition to the vaccine supply, China has also been concerned about the improvement in pandemic prevention and control capacities in the Mekong countries. On December 22, 2021, Sinopharm CNBG and the Ministry of Industry of Myanmar held a signing ceremony for the agreement on the supply of semi-finished products for COVID-19 vaccines. The cooperation between China and Myanmar on vaccine supply and procurement will effectively meet Myanmar's vaccine demand gap, enhance its epidemic prevention and control capacity, and help Myanmar gain the ability to independently produce vaccines and other biological products.

Brightness Action Lights Up the Mekong Basin

China's provision of vaccines to the Mekong countries from 2021—2022

Donor	Recipient	Time	Number of vaccines (10,000 doses)
Chinese government ➡	Laotian government	2021.02.08	30
		2021.04.01	80
		2021.04.26	30
		2021.06.14	50
		2021.10.13	100
		2021.11.25	250
		2022.01.25	150
		2022.02.14	42.32
		2021.08.23	

(continued)

(continued)

From	To	Date	Value
Chinese government	Cambodian government	2021.02.07	60
		2021.03.31	70
		2021.04.28	40
		2021.06.08	50
		2021.08.01	100
		2021.10.14	200
		2021.11.17	200
		2022.03.29	500
Chinese government	Myanmar government	2021.05.02	50
		2021.07.24	200
		2021.09.03	100
		2021.10.14	200
		2021.11.12	300
		2021.12.22	100
		2022.03.10	100
		2021.05.17	50
Chinese government	Thai government	2021.06.05	50
		2021.11.12	150
		2021.12.09	20
Chinese government	Thai monarchy	2021.06.20	50
Chinese government	Vietnamese government	2021.09.30	
		2021.08.23	20

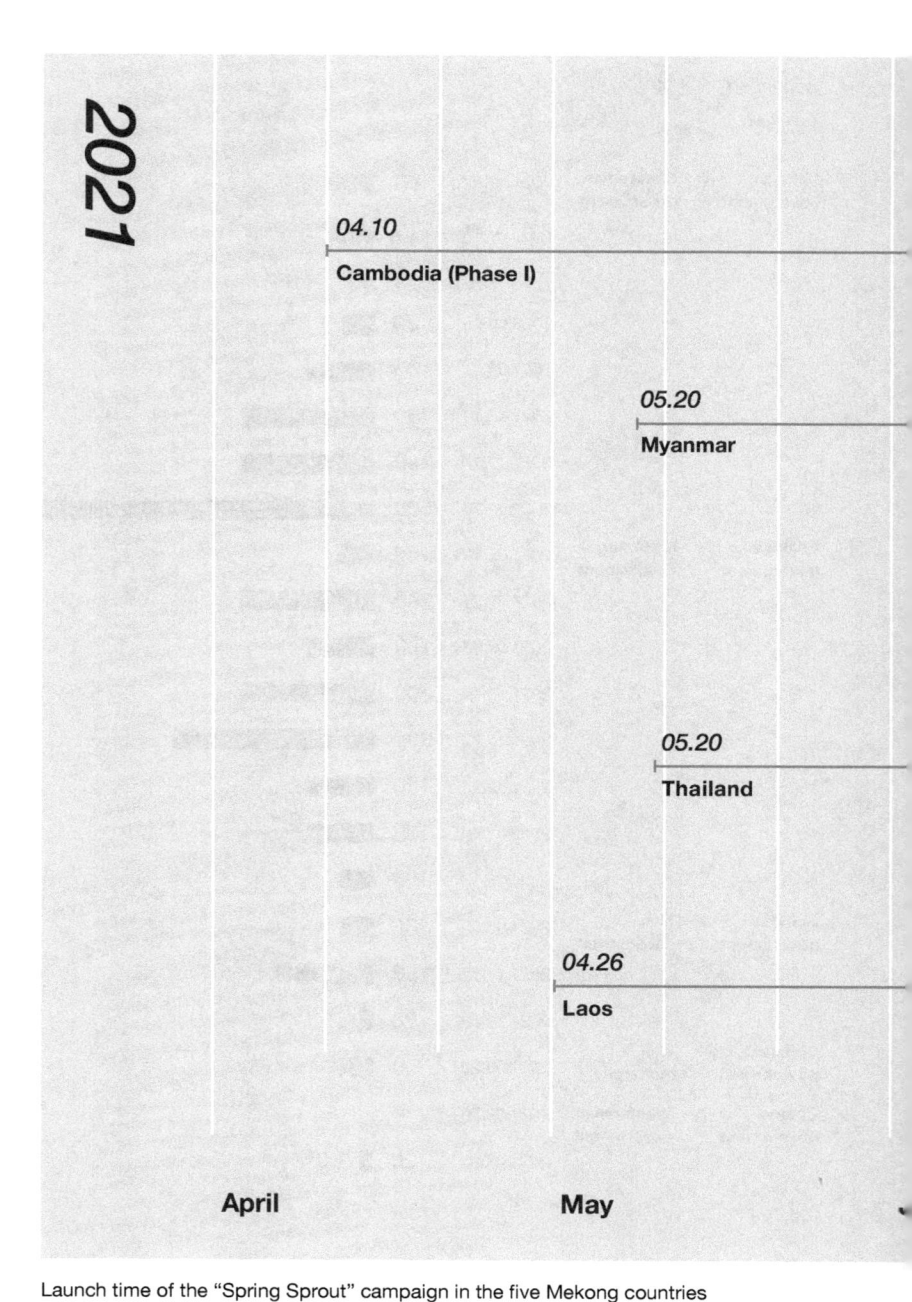

Launch time of the "Spring Sprout" campaign in the five Mekong countries

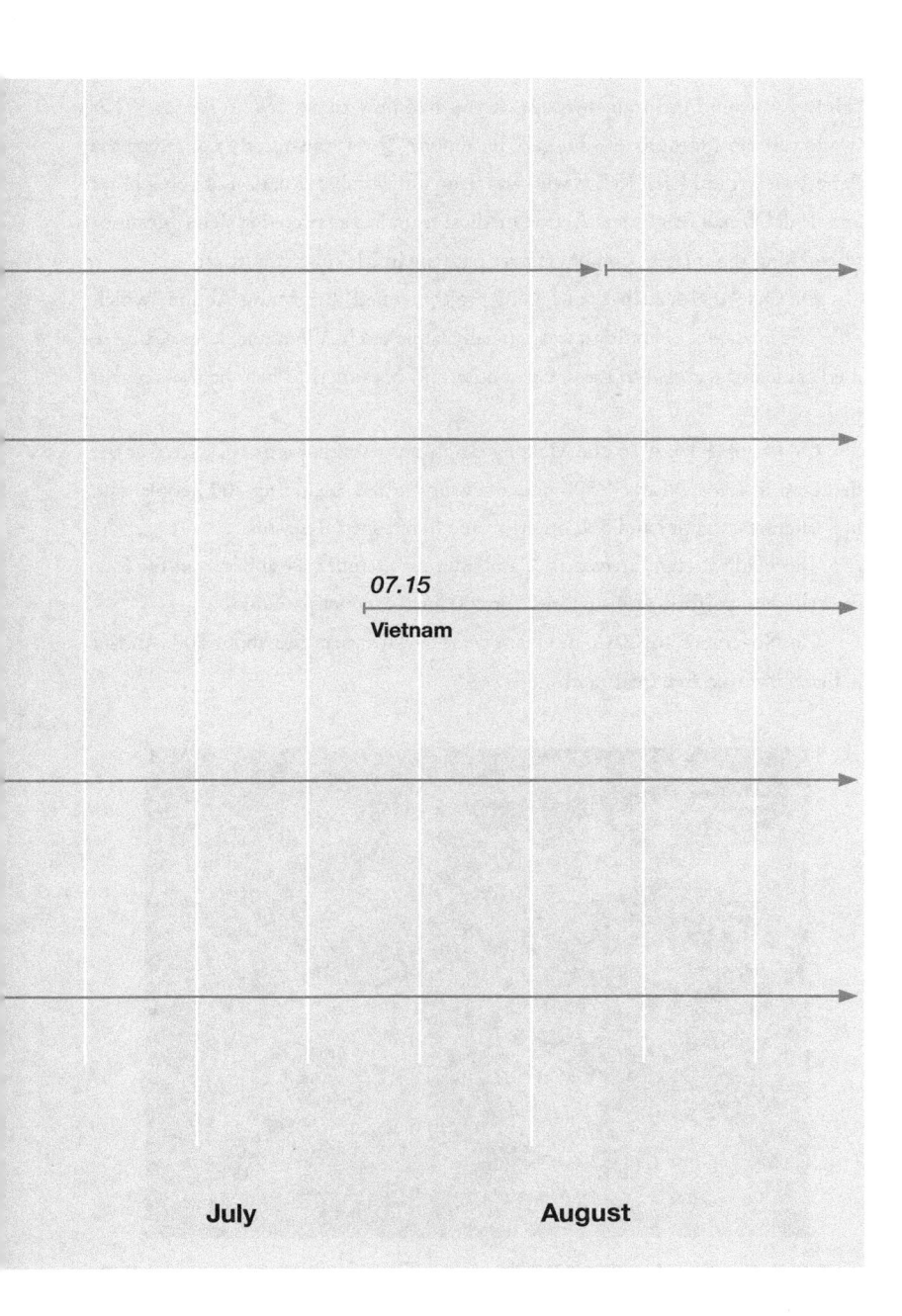

07.15
Vietnam

July   August

"How you would use your own eyes if you had only three days to see ... What would you most want to let your gaze rest upon?" This is the question posed by the American writer Helen Keller, who was in an unfavorable situation of being blind and deaf. China's Brightness Action medical team has answered Helen's questions by catching the imagination of cataract patients in Mekong countries.

On October 14, 2016, the Mekong project named "Brightness Action," which offers free cataract operations, was officially launched in Vientiane, Laos. Chinese medical teams traveled to Laos, Cambodia, and Myanmar to help patients regain their sight.

On October 14, 2016, the Mekong Brightness Action program, started at the first stop in Laos. Nearly 1,500 patients were treated, including 200 people who had cataract surgeries and 500 others were offered special glasses.

The medical team arrived in Cambodia on October 24 and stayed for four days there to perform free surgeries for 200 local cataract patients.

On November 16, 2016, the team went to Myanmar and about 200 cataract patients received free treatment.

China's Brightness Action program in the Mekong River Basin brought myopic lens to local students, Phnom Penh, Cambodia

In the first phase of the Mekong Brightness Action program, free cataract surgeries were performed in Cambodia, Laos, and Myanmar, with more than 3,000 patients being examined and treated, and a total of about 800 patients regained their sight. The success of this action, however, was not at the end, but at the beginning of the journey to brightness.

From September 2016 to December 2018, the Brightness Action program carried out surgeries for 1,000 Cambodian patients in five sessions.

On November 16, 2016, and August 9, 2017, the Yunnan Myanmar Brightness Action team operated on 400 patients in Myanmar. By 2017, more than 10 Chinese medical and charitable organizations had conducted 27 Brightness Action programs by opening charity clinics in Myanmar, successfully performing cataract surgeries for nearly 6,000 patients, and restoring hope for thousands of Myanmar families.

On August 21, 2018, and November 22, 2019, the Brightness Action program launched by Yunnan Province in Vientiane brought light to 200 cataract patients. The program not only restored the patients' vision, but the heartfelt gratitude of the patients and the friendly exchanges between both sides also brightened the hearts of the medical team.

"We both feel hopeful about coming to the surgery today! The Chinese doctor was so well-versed that I just felt a hint of pain, and the surgery was quickly over. I'm looking forward to removing the bandage tomorrow, and I hope to be able to see it as clearly as before!"

"Thank you very much. I wish you good health, and Buddha will bless you."

"Without you, I'd still be living in the dark. In our hearts, the Hainan Medical Team means light!"

"It's all right now. I can use both of my eyes to see clearly. I can help with the chores at home and no longer be a burden for my children …"

Behind all these figures are pairs of shining eyes, and behind each act of gratitude is the desire for a better life. In the future, the brightness campaign will continue to bring light to more people!

Safeguarding the Border

The pandemic prevention and control measures in border areas were extremely complex and heavy because of the high mobility and sophistication of people and cargo. Among the Mekong countries, Vietnam, Myanmar, and Laos share a border with China. Once there is an outbreak at the border, both of the two neighboring countries will be affected seriously. To tackle this, safeguarding the border from both sides was an urgent task and a protracted battle as well. In the Three Kingdoms Period of China (AD 220–280), Zhuge Liang had three smart plans to win battles. Now, there are three plans to fight the pandemic at the border as well.

The first plan: It takes a good blacksmith to forge good tools. We need to consolidate pandemic prevention measures on both sides of the border to ensure the minimization of domestic cases.

To help others is to help oneself. When the epidemic was serious in Myanmar in 2021, China not only donated several batches of vaccines to the country but also paid extra attention to strengthening epidemic prevention and control measures and vaccine supplies in the border areas of the two countries.

Myanmar's Kachin and Shan States are adjacent to China's Yunnan Province. To help control the epidemic in the area, the Chinese Ministry of Foreign Affairs donated a total of RMB 4.52 million worth of antivirus supplies to Kachin and Shan States respectively, on August 27 and September 5, 2021, through channels

Ruili Border Inspection Station makes every effort to fight against the epidemic

under the Agreement on Management and Cooperation in China-Myanmar Border Areas.

The second plan: Both sides communicate effectively to share information and contribute joint efforts to truly implement pandemic control measures in border areas.

The video-conferences on pandemic prevention work are an important com-munication platform for China and Myanmar to respond jointly to COVID-19. Although face-to-face communication was not possible, the need for both sides to jointly control the pandemic together has allowed for effective information sharing on the screen.

Although confined to the screen, the exchange between China and Myanmar through videoconferences was not limited. Looking back, the two countries reviewed the progress that was made in joint prevention and control of the pandemic at the border. Looking at the present, the two sides assessed the developmental trends of the pandemic and its impact on the border areas between them. Looking ahead, both countries jointly came up with a vision for future actions—to apply the bilateral joint prevention and control mechanism, strengthen cooperation in fighting the epidemic, and make every effort to cut off the cross-border spread of the pandemic and serve the bigger picture of pandemic prevention and the development of people's livelihood in the border areas, by continuously applying preventive measures and promoting vaccinations to build immunity, etc.

Lao Herbal Pharmacopoeia

Lead researcher Jing Xianghong is giving a lecture on "The Clinical Study of Acupuncture and Moxibustion—Where East Meets West"

The third plan: Adapt border management techniques according to specific situations, trying to synchronize the customs clearance of goods and the pandemic prevention and control procedures. Joint border prevention and control should ensure both the safety of people's lives and the stability of economic activities.

In July 2021, the border trade between China and Myanmar had to be suspended in Ruili, Yunnan Province, due to the serious epidemic, causing great difficulties in the flow of goods between the two countries. During the suspension of the border trade port, the Chinese embassy and consulate in Myanmar did a lot of facilitation work to strengthen cooperation between China and Myanmar in fighting the pandemic. Preventive measures were initially implemented, and China donated one million doses of specifically to northern Myanmar in a targeted manner, aided the construction of the COVID-19 treatment center in the Muse district of Shan State, explored non-contact transportation methods, such as using containers and cranes to deliver cross-border cargo, etc. On November 26, the Mangman border passage of Wanding Port officially resumed import and export cargo clearances, marking the formal restoration of China-Myanmar border trade, which had been suspended since July due to the impact of the pandemic in Ruili.

Traditional Chinese Medicine and Chinese Herbal Medicine Enter the Lancang-Mekong Region

In recent years, projects such as Chinese Materia Medica and Chinese Acupuncture-Moxibustion benefiting the Lancang-Mekong countries have sparked a wave of mania for Traditional Chinese Medicine in the Lancang-Mekong region.

Medicine is used for healing, and Chinese herbal medicine is an important medium for traditional treatments. Therefore, in order to produce medicine, one must first have some knowledge about herbs. Shen Nong tasted hundreds of herbs to learn about the properties of medicines in the world. Nowadays, although there is no need to personally test the toxicity of herbs, the Chinese Academy of Chinese Medical Sciences still conducts on-site research to learn about medicinal planting and the Chinese medicine industry in the Mekong countries, compiling data on medicinal plants and taking the first step toward "knowing the herbs."

In ancient times, Li Shizhen wrote the "Compendium of Materia Medica" to prescribe medicine for specific symptoms. The pharmacopeia that was formulated is the basis for Traditional Chinese Medicine to treat diseases and save lives, as well as an important medium for Traditional Chinese Medicine and Chinese herbal medicine to be accepted and understood by the five Mekong countries. Today, China and Laos have jointly compiled the first quality standard for herbal medicines in Laos: Lao Herbal Pharmacopoeia. The development of Traditional Chinese Medicine in the Lancang-Mekong countries is now "entering a good phase."

Those who study medicine must understand meridians and acupoints, which are the foundation of acupuncture and moxibustion in Traditional Chinese Medicine and the main content of the project for Traditional Chinese Medicine acupuncture in the Lancang-Mekong region. In the three online live courses for the project held by the Institute of Acupuncture and Moxibustion at the China Academy of Chinese Medical Sciences, more than 1,600 people from the five countries where the Mekong River is situated, have learned not only the basic theory of meridians in Traditional Chinese Medicine but also specific treatments such as acupuncture techniques for treating headaches and applying acupoint patches.

Doctors and healthcare professionals dedicate their lives to helping people and saving their lives with compassionate hearts and superb medical skills. To help Traditional Chinese Medicine play a more significant role, a group of practitioners who really understand the theory of Traditional Chinese Medicine are needed. In recent years, China has conducted online training for more than 700 traditional medical practitioners and students from the Lancang-Mekong countries, and the team is growing.

The efficacy of Traditional Chinese Medicine has been fully demonstrated and China has successively dispatched Traditional Chinese Medicine expert teams and medical teams, in the fight against the pandemic, to the Mekong countries. Traditional Chinese Medicine is continuously gaining attention and becoming a shining star in LMC.

Lead researcher Jing Xianghong is giving a lecture on the Clinical Study of Acupuncture and Moxibustion—Where East Meets West.

Joint Prevention and Control Measures for Cross-Border Infectious Diseases in the Lancang-Mekong Region

Due to their humid and hot climates, the Lancang-Mekong countries have always been situated in areas where diseases such as malaria and dengue fever are prevalent. We can't change the climate, but we can use the power of information technology to try to prevent the spread of diseases and promote cleanliness and hygiene in the region.

Malaria and dengue fever have brought great suffering to the people in the region. However, now, with joint prevention and control measures for vector-borne diseases in the Lancang-Mekong subregion, the six countries can benefit from informatization management such as cross-border monitoring, prediction and early warning, and information sharing, to establish an effective information network to prevent the spread of diseases.

In 2019, the joint prevention and control measures for vector-borne diseases in the Lancang-Mekong subregion deployed 19 fever clinical monitoring sites, forming a vector-borne disease prevention line in 8 prefectures and counties along the Yunnan border and generating monitoring reports on a monthly and weekly basis, as the network covers 5 provinces in northern Laos. It had also deployed 2,227 Aedes vector survey sites along the Yunnan border and 16 regional meteorological stations and trained over 200 technical personnel. Nearly 200,000 kinds of monitoring data of various types were collected, forming a data set that consists of 15 themes in 5 major categories, including mosquito and infectious disease monitoring, regional geographic data, regional meteorological data, remote sensing data, and regional social and cultural data.

On April 25, 2022, version 2.0 of the joint prevention and control measures for vector-borne diseases in the Lancang-Mekong subregion was officially launched in a series of activities for public health cooperation during the LMC Week of 2022. With the continuous progress of science and technology, the cross-border control and prevention of infectious diseases will also be continuously enhanced, entering a more efficient 2.0 era.

As one of the major infectious diseases that pose a threat to human health, AIDS is a major public health issue faced by the whole world. In order to control the spread of this disease, Guangxi and Yunnan provinces on China's border have established a disease information exchange platform with Vietnam and Myanmar.

Bordering Vietnam, Guangxi Province has achieved the effective sharing of disease information with Vietnam by training professional technical personnel at border areas, establishing a joint prevention and control mechanism, and conducting bilateral exchanges and cooperation with Lang Son, Quang Ninh, Cao Bang, and Ha Giang provinces in Vietnam.

Since 2016, starting from the establishment of a cross-border referral service site in Myanmar, the Yunnan Institute for Drug Abuse has established a China-Myanmar cross-border referral service mechanism, with support from the joint prevention and control measures for cross-border HIV/AIDS in the Lancang-Mekong region, which has preliminarily formed a high-quality "service chain" from identifying cross-border HIV-infected individuals and referring them for antiviral therapy, and implementing collaborative management strategies and techniques for HIV-infected individuals and AIDS patients.

The Lancang River

With Everlasting Mountains and Rivers, the Six Countries March toward a Shared Future

Eight years of cooperation has accumulated momentum for a new takeoff. The LMC is a collaboration concerning the six countries, concerning the future, and concerning the well-being of humans and it requires concerted, unremitting efforts, and careful nurturing. Looking ahead, there are great expectations for China and the Mekong countries to jointly open a more prosperous and peaceful future for this region. Such expectations are not only based on the influence of China's own development and progress regarding the outside world, but also on China's wisdom and solutions, such as the "LMC" and the "community that has a shared future for the Lancang-Mekong countries," which have continued to help solve regional problems. Moreover, these expectations are based on China and the Mekong countries working together to actively engage on the world stage. Despite the high mountains and treacherous rapids ahead, if the six countries of the Lancang-Mekong region work together and help each other, the "LMC" will surely overcome all difficulties and obstacles and embark on a glorious road toward a better future for the Lancang-Mekong community with a shared future.

Another "Golden Five-Year Period" for the Lancang-Mekong Region

We Can Achieve a Leap Forward and Build a Community with Common Interests

Since its establishment, the LMC has moved from being strangers to becoming familiar with each other, from knowing to supporting each other, and from generating conceptual ideas to implementing concrete actions. Increasingly, a growing number of the "fruits of Lancang-Mekong" have ripened and arrived, and carry the common dreams of the six countries. The LMC has broken through barriers, conformed to the development goals of the five Mekong countries and vividly connected the Chinese Dream with the dreams of people in these countries, which not only helps to promote economic prosperity and regional economic cooperation in the basin, but also strengthens exchanges and mutual learning among different civilizations, and has built a Lancang-Mekong community with a shared future that works hand in hand. The common future of the six countries will be a brighter one, as the interests of each country and each ethnic group are integral parts of the common interests of the people in the Lancang-Mekong region, whose interests are in return closely linked to the Lancang-Mekong community that has a shared future, in which "you are a part of me, and I am a part of you."

At present, the world economy is under increasingly downward pressure and the international situation is facing many challenges, so, no country can survive alone, and it is high time for cooperation and co-development. In the face of new challenges, the Fourth LMC Leaders' Meeting was held on December 25, 2023, and issued the Five-Year Plan of Action on LMC (2023–2027), which outlines a blueprint for the development of LMC in the new era while laying a solid foundation and framework for future cooperation.

The one who achieves great success in the world is also the one who has strategic plans. With the concept of the "Lancang-Mekong countries belonging to a community with a shared future" deeply rooted in people's minds, a magnificent blueprint carrying the beautiful vision of the Lancang-Mekong countries is gradually unfolding. To turn the blueprint into a construction plan, scientific conceptualization, and a rigorous top-level design are required. The formulation of the new five-year blueprint undoubtedly represents the best interpretation of the concept of a Lancang-Mekong community with a shared future and the pragmatic advancement of the LMC.

The next five-year action plan will become a guiding plan for the LMC to move forward from a growth period to a comprehensive development period. It will continue to promote all-round, multi-field cooperation and development among the six countries in politics, economy, sociocultural, and ecology, further expand and broaden the cooperation, injecting strong impetus into the construction of a Lancang-Mekong community with a shared future.

The Nuozhadu Hydropower Station in the Lancang River Basin

For those having the same aspirations and seeking the same goals, distance is not an obstacle. Standing at a new historical starting point, the six countries will continue to uphold neighborly friendship, vigorously promote practical cooperation in all fields, actively build the Lancang-Mekong River economic development belt, share successful experiences, jointly launch projects, and consolidate the joint forces of sub-regional development, bringing more well-being to the people in the Lancang-Mekong region. It is believed that with the joint efforts of the six countries, the LMC will become a model of sub-regional cooperation, a vivid example of building a new type of international relations, and a pioneering and testing ground for constructing a community with a shared future for humankind which will promote the "Lancang-Mekong dream" that benefits all people in the region, and turn it into a reality.

Nothing Hinders the LMC

It's hard for a loner to set off. Together, we can travel afar.

A Peaceful Lancang-Mekong Region

The current situation of the world is complicated and turbulent, and the theme of peace and development is facing great challenges. The world is changing in an unprecedented way, and in the face of various traditional and non-traditional security challenges, no country can stand alone and stay clear from threats, nor can any country realize the so-called "absolute security."

A peaceful and stable environment is indispensable for the LMC. In the "3 + 5 + X" Cooperation Framework, political security ranked the top among the three pillars, reflecting its crucial role for China and the Mekong countries.

The prerequisite for political security is mutual trust. Mutual respect, fairness, and justice, and win-win forms of cooperation are the foundations and guarantees for promoting the LMC. The community of the Lancang-Mekong countries is a peaceful community with a shared future. Over the years, China has always adhered to a secutiry philosophy of being sharing, comprehensive, cooperative, and sustainable, and is committed to building a Lancang-Mekong sub-region where countries respect each other's core interests and resolve their disputes and conflicts peacefully. These ideas and actions have been set in accordance with the historical view of society development, bringing together the greatest number of conventions on security and development issues among the people of the six Mekong countries, echoing the common voice of all the peace-loving people, which shines brightly for peace in a turbulent and fast-changing world.

The pursuit of peace should be the guidance for our actions. The six Lancang-Mekong countries are interconnected, so peace is an inherent need to build a community with a shared future. Only by abandoning the hegemonic approach of jungle laws, all forms of cold war thinking, and the zero-sum mindset, can we create a fair and just security framework for co-building and sharing that will lead to long-lasting peace. We believe that as long as we maintain regional peace in our convictions and never forget to make peace a top priority, we will be able to pave a peaceful road in the region and find a path to build a community of a shared future with long-lasting peace in the Mekong countries, so that the torch of peace will be passed down through generations and the bell of security will ring loudly on earth.

A Secure Lancang-Mekong Region

Over the past eight years, the LMC has gone through an extraordinary journey in terms of security and has made significant achievements. The concept of cooperation in security has been enriched and developed, the mechanism has gradually matured, and practical cooperation has been broadened and expanded. With the joint efforts of the six Mekong countries, the region has maintained security and stability, which has offered favorable conditions for socioeconomic development. Synergies have been formed by joint efforts in dialogues, constructions, and sharing, establishing a new model of international relations characterized by cooperation and mutual benefit.

At present, the Mekong Basin is still facing various traditional and non-traditional security threats, but the theme of maintaining security, the pursuit of a better life by the people of the region, and the historical mission of the six countries to work together for win-win results remain unchanged. The right path should lead with the historical trend. With the further advancement of the LMC, the six countries will continue to deepen security cooperation in public health, water resources, and joint law enforcement, strengthen communication and coordination, and build a secure order of mutual trust and equality.

In the face of the sudden COVID-19 pandemic, the Lancang-Mekong countries have shown the spirit of a community with a shared future by taking practical actions in close collaborations and providing mutual support for each other, setting an example of solidarity against the pandemic. Life and health are the most important issues for human beings, yet viruses are not contained within national boundaries. Only by uniting with and helping each other can the Lancang-Mekong countries better cope with regional health and security problems.

The Mekong River

In the post-pandemic era, public health will become a new highlight of cooperation between China and the Mekong countries. Focusing on the medical and health needs of the sub-region, the LMC will bring into play the advantages of Chinese medical institutions and pandemic prevention techniques, encouraging communications and the sharing of experiences with other Lancang-Mekong countries in pandemic prevention and control. China will coordinate with the countries and jointly establish and improve, for the advancement of long-term goals, the mechanisms required for major public health emergencies. China will also actively participate in developing new mechanisms and platforms for sub-regional cooperation in the medical care and public health sectors, committing itself to improving the health and medical care of people in the sub-region.

With a shared future, China and the Mekong countries watch out for each other. In 2011, the world was shocked by the tragic Mekong River massacre on October 5. In order to maintain the safety and stability of the Mekong waterway, China, Laos, Myanmar, and Thailand creatively established a mechanism of Law Enforcement Security Cooperation in the Mekong River Basin, and took the lead in practical cooperation by initiating a joint patrol made up of representatives from China, Laos, Myanmar, and Thailand on the Mekong River. Today, China, Laos, Myanmar, and Thailand have gone through 11 years of joint patrols and cooperative law enforcement on the Mekong River, and as of December 22, 2023, 136 joint patrols have been initiated. In the process of building the Lancang-Mekong community with a shared future, China, Laos, Myanmar, and Thailand will always uphold the Asian security concept of establishing common interests, adopting comprehensive measures, with cooperation and sustainability in mind to actively promote the LMC spirit of mutual support, mutual respect and tolerance, equality, and mutual benefit. We will work together to curb all kinds of illegal and criminal acts in the Mekong River Basin, safeguard the safety of international shipping and the legitimate rights and interests of the people in the basin, and create a new model of international law enforcement and cooperation in security.

A tree can grow to 100 feet because its roots are deep; the sea can be 10,000 feet deep because small streams converge into it. Water resources are important natural resources and valuable assets for the survival of the people in the member countries of the LMC. At present, the Mekong countries are in a stage of rapid socioeconomic development, and the demand for water resources in industrialization and urbanization is ever-growing. At the same time, the six countries also face challenges such as frequent floods and droughts, damage to water ecosystems in some areas, increased water pollution, and uncertainties caused by climate change. Besides, there are problems such as the backward water infrastructure construction to varying degrees and the water governance capacity needs to be improved. It is an important responsibility of the governments of the six countries to promote sustainable socioeconomic development that benefits the people of each member country through sustainable use, effective management, and protection of water resources.

Looking back, the original intention of the LMC remains unchanged; looking forward, the mission is on our shoulders. The six Lancang-Mekong countries will continue to share the development opportunities of the basin in the spirit of solidarity, equality and consultation, and work together to address the water-related challenges to the sustainable development of the river basin, to promote cooperation in water resources to a new level. On this basis, we will have more discussions on water resources policy, facilitate technical cooperation, share information and data to jointly enhance the sustainable use, effective management and protection of water resources in the six countries, to promote and guarantee sustainable economic and social development that benefits the people of the Mekong countries. The six Mekong countries should also take into account the specific conditions of water resources for each country, note each other's concerns, and uphold the principle of "dialogue, construction and sharing" to make the LMWRC a flagship model of the LMC and turn the Lancang-Mekong River into a river of friendship, cooperation and prosperity.

A Prosperous Lancang-Mekong Region

When the pandemic intertwined and overlapped with profound changes that haven't been seen in a century, cooperation for the means of achieving development is the common desire of all countries in the world. Thanks to the efforts of the six Lancang-Mekong countries, a large number of high-standard, sustainable and people-friendly infrastructure projects have made significant progress, providing a strong impetus to the economic development of the Mekong Basin. With the launch of the China–Laos Railway as a rallying trumpet, a large number of cooperative construction projects are progressing smoothly and some have achieved substantial results. On December 3, 2021, the China–Laos Railway officially opened for operation, running from Kunming, Yunnan Province, China to Vientiane, the capital of Laos, and as part of the Central Line of the Trans–Asian Railway, which will also be extended to Bangkok, the capital of Thailand in the future—the China–Thailand Railway is another project that is worth looking forward to.

Development is the master key to solving all problems. Promoting the LMC and focusing on development can maximize the potential of the countries in the region and achieve economic integration, development linkages and sharing. The six Lancang-Mekong countries have their own advantages in terms of their market scales and natural resources, providing strong complementarity, tremendous potential, and broad prospects for cooperation. On the basis of fully accommodating the interests and concerns of all parties, the Lancang-Mekong countries will forge a consensus, translate it into action, and create more visible results, drawing on each other's strengths while promoting common prosperity and development. The LMC will continue to focus on regional interconnection and infrastructure construction for the benefit of the people.

China has established close economic and trade ties with the Mekong countries, which have strongly contributed to the economic and industrial development of each country. The five Mekong countries have become China's important trading partners, and the steady and positive development of the regional economy demonstrates the firm confidence and resilience of bilateral cooperation. Looking ahead, there will be promising results stemming from bilateral cooperation in regard to the economy and trade, and there will be more areas available for cooperation. Deepening practical cooperation in various fields such as trade, agriculture, investment, and poverty alleviation is an important way to achieve win-win situations. In addition, cross-border economic cooperative zones play a key role in the cross-border economy. Under the new trends of the booming digital economy and the reshaping of cross-border economic cooperation zones by the RCEP, it is reasonable to believe that cross-border economic cooperation zones will present new highlights. The LMC will become a new platform for economic development and a driving force for the regional cross-border economy of the countries along the river, helping the countries to achieve leapfrog development.

The pandemic has partially disconnected the global industrial chain, highlighting the fragility and inadequacy of the current system. Even when presented with this challenge, Lancang-Mekong countries have achieved rapid, comprehensive, and remarkable development in economic interactions, and both sides have become important economic partners for each other, which has laid a solid foundation for production capacity cooperation. Promoting industrial development and upgrading industries is a long-term task for the six countries. They have enormous demands in infrastructure construction and accelerated industrialization. Through production capacity cooperation, the economic and trade connections of the six Lancang-Mekong countries can be further strengthened, and the confidence and enthusiasm coming from the industries on both sides can be boosted. When the RCEP came into effect, the customs clearance procedure was more efficient within the region, and the market was further expanded, which promoted closer cooperation among the member countries and created greater business opportunities. Undoubtedly, the signing of the RCEP will transform the regional economic integration process into a brand-new stage and become an important driving force for a regional economic recovery in the post-pandemic era.

The road to shared prosperity may be long, but it is worth looking forward to.

An Open Lancang-Mekong Region

The LMC insists on openness and inclusiveness and opposes exclusivity, providing an important platform for the building of a community with a shared future in the Mekong countries. In the LMC family, different systems and civilizations are accommodated without an ideological bias; every partner is equal regardless of economic size, and no political conditions are attached to every form of cooperation. For any cooperative initiative in the region that is conducive to strengthening connectivity and achieving common development, the LMC holds an open attitude and advances mutual cooperation and mutual benefits. It has been proven time and again that the LMC is a sunny path where common development can be attained and a large garden where different kinds of flowers bloom together.

The six Lancang-Mekong countries have consistently upheld the principles of multilateralism and win-win cooperation, aiming to jointly address challenges and enhance the well-being of the people in the region. The LMC has always adhered to the principles of openness and inclusiveness, focusing on mutual promotion and coordinated development with other regional and sub-regional cooperation mechanisms such as ASEAN, The Ayeyawady-Chao Phraya-Mekong Economic Cooperation Strategy (ACMECS), the Greater Mekong Subregion Economic Cooperation (GMS), and the Mekong River Commission (MRC). At the same time, the LMC welcomes the active participation of the World Bank, the Asian Infrastructure Investment Bank, the Asian Development Bank, and other institutions to jointly promote the building of the ASEAN community and the process of regional economic integration.

National friendships are more prevalent in interpersonal bonds, which rely on effective communication. Over the past eight years, the Mekong countries have held various cultural exchanges in a wide range of fields, which have enhanced mutual understanding and recognition and laid a solid foundation for the LMC. The LMC has opened the window of interaction among people of different nationalities and written a historical chapter in the progression of civilization. The profound civilization heritage and inclusive cultural philosophy of the LMC provide a platform for countries along the river to meet each other, learn from each other, and promote in-depth exchanges among people from different countries, cultures, and historical backgrounds, so that the people of the river basin can sense, integrate and connect with each other at new heights, and jointly promote the building of a community with a shared future for the Lancang-Mekong countries.

Developing interpersonal bonds starts with the youth, and exchanges among young people are the most important part of the LMC to build a strong people-to-people bond. It is interesting, meaningful and significant for the youth of the six Mekong countries to look at the world with an appreciative and open perspective, and to promote the coexistence and exchange of different civilizations. In the Second Five-Year Plan of the Lancang-Mekong Youth Exchange and Cooperation program, we will jointly promote the establishment of youth cooperation centers at all levels, open up more cooperation channels, and plan more high-quality youth cooperation projects. We will facilitate off-line communication with online exchanges, using the Internet to amplify the communications among the young people. We will also promote education cooperation to expand the scale of exchange students that we send to each other, improve the quality of cooperation regarding school operations, and make the Lancang-Mekong Youth Exchange a catalyst for cooperation between schools and local authorities, to achieve leapfrog development of the LMC. The seeds of civilization are being sown on the LMC path through humanistic exchanges and mutual learning.

A Beautiful Lancang-Mekong Region

The vitality released by the LMC in the new journey is inseparable from its green background. Over the past eight years, the six Mekong countries have broadened green practices and made positive progress in green development based on the common goal of building a beautiful home. The profound integration of green engineering, green transportation, green consumption, etc., has taken a new step in concept innovation, mutual reference, and practical cooperation. Green has become the representative color of the LMC.

A drop of water does not make an ocean, and a single tree does not make a forest. Building an ecological planet and caring for our green home won't be possible without the active actions of all the countries. The Lancang-Mekong Environmental Cooperation Strategy and the Green Lancang-Mekong Initiative have set specific tasks around biodiversity conservation, air quality improvement, demonstration of clean water projects, sustainable infrastructure, and so on, indicating the pursuit of green development by the LMC in the future. Whether it is infrastructure construction, energy cooperation, the green industry, trade, scientific and technological innovations, establishment of standards, etc., green and sustainable development should be placed in an important position. The six Lancang-Mekong countries share a common vision and work together to integrate the concept of green development and mutually beneficial cooperation into all areas, setting a model for the world to take a steady and reliable path of green development.

Green transformation and the upgrading of industries means that we need to abandon certain traditional sectors with high energy consumption and high emissions and turn to energy-saving, environmentally friendly, green, and low-carbon directions. High energy consumption expires when new equipment comes to the fore, which is undoubtedly the unavoidable path for the Green Mekong Initiative. The six Lancang-Mekong countries will work closely together to create an environment-friendly and innovation-driven economic growth model to help the region reconstruct itself in a better, greener, and smarter fashion in the post-pandemic era. To this end, the Lancang-Mekong region will make every effort to develop a Bio-Circular-Green economy, promote innovation, and build innovation corridors and a network of R&D centers to support the development of economic and industrial zones in the border areas of the Lancang-Mekong countries. The prospect of the LMC is very promising, as it has seized and expanded opportunities for green cooperation.

Unite and progress together, the Lancang-Mekong countries will have a brighter future. The LMC is not only a path to prosperity and development, but also a beautiful road of green civilization.

Although the LMC started late, it has shown great vitality and strong momentum in just eight years. The fundamental reason is that it always follows the philosophy of development priority, equality and consultation, pragmatism and efficiency, open-mindedness, and inclusiveness, and it always adheres to the principles of mutual consultation, common construction, and sharing. Now that the new golden Five-Year Plan of Action on LMC has begun, cooperation in various fields has been geared up at full pace in a broader and deeper manner. The cooperation will deepen the five priority sectors and continue to expand the "X" to strengthen cooperation in education, health, poverty reduction, and women's and youth affairs so as to enrich the connotation of the LMC and contribute to the sustainable development of the region.

The trumpet of the LMC is sonorous in the six countries, and LMC projects have been widely praised. The values and concept of development embodied in the LMC are in line with the inherent demand for building a human community with a shared future, as well as the strong desire and expectation of the people living in the region to share development opportunities and create better lives. Undoubtedly, as time goes by, the LMC mechanism will further demonstrate its strong vitality and creativity. It will contribute to the lasting peace, universal security, common prosperity, and an open, inclusive, clean, and beautiful home, and an ultimate vision of building a community with a shared future for the Lancang-Mekong countries.

ABOUT THE EDITOR

Lu Guangsheng is the Dean of the School of International Relations at Yunnan University, Director of the Center for Peripheral Diplomacy Studies, and Deputy Director of the Lancang-Mekong Cooperation Research Center. He is a recipient of the National Talent Project, the State Council's Special Allowance, and is recognized as a "Yunling Scholar" and a leading young academic in Yunnan Province.